Al Barkow is editor-at-large of *Golf Illustrated* and the former editor-in-chief of *Golf Illustrated* and *Golf*. He has been a freelance writer for sports magazines, including *Sports Illustrated*, *Golf Digest*, and *Golf Journal*. He is the author of *Golf's Golden Grind: A History of the Tour* and *Gettin' to the Dance Floor: An Oral History of American Golf*. He was a contributing writer to *Golf Legends*, *20th Century Golf Chronicle*, *Best of Golf*, and *The Love of Golf*.

David Barrett is a senior editor at *Golf*. He was a contributing writer to *Golf Legends*, *20th Century Golf Chronicle*, *Golf in America: The First One Hundred Years*, *The PGA Championship: 1916–1984*, *Best of Golf*, and *The Love of Golf*.

Ken Janke is the author of *Golf Is a Funny Game* and a contributing writer to *The Love of Golf*. He serves as chairman of the Michigan Golf Hall of Fame.

CONTENTS

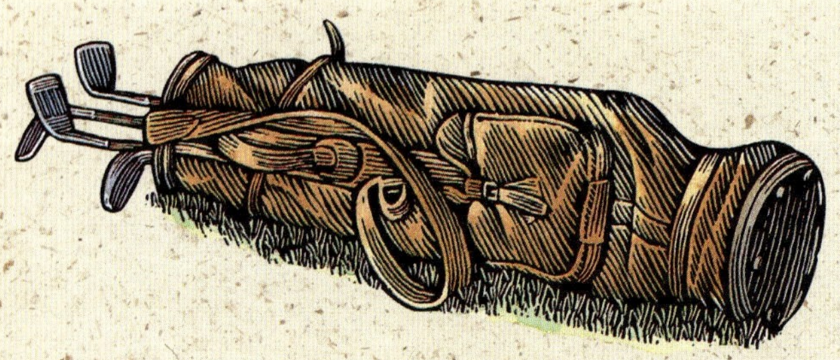

The Wit & Wisdom of GOLF

Contributing Writers
Al Barkow
David Barrett
Ken Janke

Cover Illustration
Glenn Fuller

Illustrators
Keith Ward
John Zielinski
Mark McIntosh

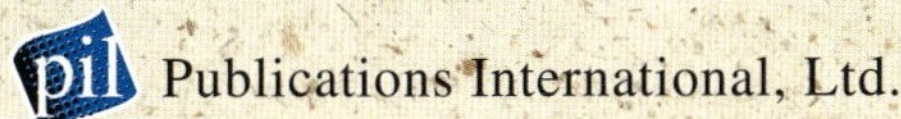

Publications International, Ltd.

Louis Weber, CEO
Publications International, Ltd.
7373 North Cicero Avenue
Lincolnwood, Illinois 60712

Manufactured in China.

8 7 6 5 4 3 2 1

ISBN-13: 978-1-4127-1388-7

ISBN-10: 1-4127-1388-9

Library of Congress Control Number: 2006935730

Hitting the Links

IN COMPILING QUOTATIONS for use in *The Wit & Wisdom of Golf,* David Barrett said, "It's easy to find quotes for 'The Trials of Golf' chapter. It's 'The Joys of Golf' that I'm having trouble with."

Indeed, when the voices of golf speak, defeatism often underlines their words. As J. C. Snead lamented, "The peaks do not seem to last as long as the valleys in this game."

Golf is the sports world's paradox. It lures us in with its peaceful settings, fresh air, sweet smells, and the occasional thrill of a great shot. But after we spend four hours in the sun, the game begins to play Twister with our insides and gnaws on our minds like a squirrel does an acorn. "Golf is a bloodless sport," said Dick Schaap, "if you don't count ulcers." Ben Crenshaw agrees. "Golf is the hardest game in the world," said Gentle Ben. "There's no way you can ever get it. Just when you think you do, the game jumps up and puts you in your place."

The Wit & Wisdom of Golf covers all aspects of the sport. One chapter reports on "The Players" and another "The Courses." The book explores the game's ups ("The Joys of Golf") and its downs ("The Trials of Golf"). It gets inside players' heads ("The Mental Game") and puts the game into a larger perspective ("The Big Picture"). It offers sage words of wisdom ("Professional Advice") and terrific one-liners ("Wisecracks"). These quotes and anecdotes are irresistible treats, sure to inspire many smiles, occasional chuckles, and frequent nods of agreement when a golf truism hits close to home.

Yet, perhaps because the participants struggle so mightily with this wretched game, the golf quotations often breathe with heavy sighs. "Oh, hang it!" cried Sir Walter Simpson. "With so many things to be thought of all at once, steady play is impossible." Even some of "The Joys of Golf" quotations are as much negative as positive. Said Henry Longhurst: "The most exquisitely satisfying act in the world of golf is that of throwing a club."

Actually, the funniest quotes in the book are those that drip with sarcasm. After hacking through the heavy grass of Carnoustie during the 1953 British Open, the great Ben Hogan quipped: "I've got a lawnmower back in Texas. I'll send it over." And when one golfer called his Scottish caddie the worst bag-toter in the entire world, the caddie retorted: "No sir. We couldn't 'ave a coincidence like that." Mean-spirited words, but cheerfully amusing!

You'll discover that one golf irony contrasts with another: The game of golf seems to promise great fun and joy but, in the end, leads to frustration and heartbreak. In contrast, the musings on the game seem despondent on the surface but, inevitably, bring smiles to our faces and comfort to our hearts.

The Joys of Golf

"The most important thing for golfers of all ages and handicaps is not that they should play golf well, but that they should play it cheerfully."

—H. J. Whigham

No Putts in a Round

ONE OF THE great characters in golf was Murray "Moe" Norman, who was originally from Kitchener, Ontario. He primarily played in Canada, although he made a brief stab at the PGA Tour. He had an outstanding record in his native country, having won 54 amateur and professional tournaments including two Canadian Amateurs and two Canadian PGA titles. At one time Moe held 33 course records, 17 of them being set the first time he had ever seen the course. The Royal Canadian Golf Association finally recognized his golfing genius by inducting Norman into its Hall of Fame in 1995.

In the 1969 Quebec Open, Norman came to the final hole needing a birdie to win the championship outright and a par to get in a playoff. Moe hit the par-5 in two and proceeded to four-putt. The next day, he was playing a practice round at Pinegrove for the Canadian Open. On the 10th, a par-3, some golf writers asked him about his putting. Moe didn't answer until he hit his shot. While it was still in the air, he said, "I'm not putting today." The shot went straight into the cup for a hole in one.

"Golf is 20 percent mechanics and technique. The other 80 percent is philosophy, humor, tragedy, romance, melodrama, companionship, cussedness, and conversation."

—Grantland Rice

"Golf combines two favorite American pastimes: taking long walks and hitting things with a stick."

—P. J. O'Rourke, *Modern Manners*

"The game can be played in company or alone. Robinson Crusoe on his island, with his man Friday as a caddie, could have realized the golfer's dream of perfect happiness—a fine day, a good course, and a clear green."

—Henry E. Howland

Sammy's Two New Clubs

When Sam Snead made his first trip to the West Coast segment of the PGA Tour in 1937, at the age of 24, he had only a little experience in tournament golf—a few events in his native West Virginia as well as in Florida and the Bahamas—and did not have a very good set of clubs. The driver he'd been using was a particular problem. It had a very flexible shaft, and for a golfer with Snead's inherent power, the shaft caused him to be pretty wild off the tee.

On the practice tee at the Los Angeles Open before the tournament began, Snead's prospects improved considerably when he pulled a driver out of the bag of Henry Picard, one of the best players on the circuit at the time. It was one of a few drivers in Picard's bag. Snead waggled the club a few times and felt an immediate difference. The shaft was much firmer. "God, this is good," Snead said, and Picard told him to take it and play with it. "My driving improved 40 percent right then and there," Snead recalled.

Snead then went to the practice putting green where he ran into a friend named Leo Walper, who wanted to putt Sam for a quarter a hole. Snead said he didn't have a putter with him, and Walper told him to get one out of his bag. Taking a look,

Snead unexpectedly found a model of Bobby Jones's Calamity Jane. Giving it a try, he made three aces in a row. With that, Walper decided that he'd lost enough quarters and put an end to the contest. He also offered to sell Snead the club for $3.50, and Snead jumped at the chance. He felt confident now that the two most important clubs a golfer can have—the driver and the putter—were quality clubs safely in his bag. Two weeks later, Snead won the Oakland Open, one of more than 100 events he would win during his fabled career.

"In so many English sports, something flying or running has to be killed or injured; golf calls for no drop of blood from any living creature."

—Henry Leach

"Golf: a game in which you claim the privileges of age, and retain the playthings of childhood."

—Samuel Johnson

Water Hazard

During the time that Walter Hagen, Jr., was on the Notre Dame golf team, the unofficial coach was Al Watrous. Frequently, Watrous would drive from Oakland Hills Country Club near Detroit to South Bend, Indiana, to give lessons and work with each of the team members. There were no expressways in the late 1930s and early '40s, so driving down afforded the opportunity to see some lovely lakes.

On one trip, Al stopped to stretch his legs in an area overlooking a lake below. There was one lonely angler in a rowboat facing the other way with his line in the water. Al figured he was a long iron away. Watrous and his car were hidden by some trees, so he opened the trunk, pulled out a 3-iron, and hit some balls aiming to the right side of the man. He rifled a shot that landed exactly where he was aiming.

The angler was sure a big one had just broken the water. He quickly pulled the line from the left side of the boat and dropped it near the ripples in the water. Al waited about a minute and hit another shot, which landed on the other side of the boat. Of course, the man quickly changed positions and threw the line in the new area where the "fish" had jumped. Watrous continued the exercise two or three more times, then placed the club back in the car and continued on his way. It would have been fun to hear the stories the angler told that evening about the big one that got away.

"Golf is so popular simply because it is the best game in the world in which to be bad."

—A. A. Milne

"It is almost impossible to remember how tragic a place the world is when one is playing golf."

—Robert Lynd

"The fascinations of golf can only be learned by experience. It is difficult to explain them. It has its humorous and its serious side. It can be begun as soon as you can walk, and once begun it is continued as long as you can see."

—Henry E. Howland

The Fat Man Who Broke 100

REX BEACH WAS a popular writer on many subjects during the 1920s and '30s, but he had a special affinity for golf. He thought the "average golfer" enjoyed the game far more than low handicappers and professionals, and to make his point he recalled entering the locker room of a club where he was to play. He saw, as he put it, "a globular little man, pink-faced and beaming." Gathered around the man were well-wishers offering their congratulations. It was his first time below 100, and Beach saw in his face a joy he rarely noticed among professionals. In fact, Beach wrote, "He glowed, he expanded until he had fewer wrinkles than a raisin; he was a boy again."

"WITH A FINE sea view, and a clear course in front of him, the golfer should find no difficulty in dismissing all worries from his mind."

—A. J. BALFOUR

"YOU'RE ONLY HERE for a short visit. Don't hurry. Don't worry. And be sure to smell the flowers along the way."

—WALTER HAGEN

"GOLF IS FULLY as companionable an amusement as it can be a solitary one."

—BERNARD DARWIN

"GOLF, THOU ART a gentle spirit; we owe thee much!"

—H. B. FARNIE

"A TOLERABLE DAY, a tolerable green, a tolerable opponent supply, or ought to supply, all that any reasonably constituted human being should require in the way of entertainment."

—A. J. BALFOUR

Golf and Sex

TWO GOLFING FRIENDS were standing side by side hitting balls on a practice range, and at one point both struck perfect shots—the balls hit solidly, their trajectories ideal and right on target. Each heaved a sigh of pleasure. They looked at each other and smiled softly. Then one said to the other, "Sometimes I think that hitting a golf ball like that is as good as sex." His friend nodded softly but emphatically, in agreement, then added, "Sometimes it's better."

"THE MAN WHO can putt is a match for anyone."

—WILLIE PARK, JR.

"LONG DRIVING, IF it be not the most deadly, is certainly the most dashing and fascinating part of the game; and of all others the principal difficulty of the golfer to acquire."

—H. B. FARNIE

"We borrowed golf from Scotland as we borrowed whiskey. Not because it is Scottish, but because it is good."

—Briton Horace Hutchinson

"Give me a millionaire with a fast backswing and I can have a very enjoyable afternoon."

—George Low

"If you're playing well, they could probably put the pin on the cart path and you could get it close."

—Mike Sullivan

"It is this constant and undying hope for improvement that makes golf so exquisitely worth the playing."

—Bernard Darwin

Sensational Journalism

GOLF WRITER DOUG Mintline of the *Flint Journal* once worked for the better part of a year to stage an annual team event between area golf clubs near that Michigan city. He ran into a number of snags along the way before all agreed that such a tournament would be possible. Doug wrote an article about the multiclub event, which was approved and scheduled to run in the Sunday edition. It was turned over to someone to write the headline, and when it appeared, the story's banner came out: "INTERCOURSE TOURNEY SET."

"GOLF IS AN indispensable adjunct to high civilization."

—ANDREW CARNEGIE

"I PLAY IN the low 80s. If it's any hotter than that, I don't play."

—JOE E. LEWIS

"GOLF IS IN the interest of good health and good manners. It promotes self-restraint and affords a chance to play the man and act the gentleman."

—WILLIAM TAFT

"REAL GOLFERS GO to work to relax."

—GEORGE DILLON

"THE GREAT STUMBLING block in the way of all players, veterans and recruits, is excitement."

—H. B. FARNIE

"GOLF AND SEX are about the only things you can enjoy without being good at it."

—JIMMY DEMARET

Breaking 100 the Hard Way

SCORING A 63 on the front nine didn't exactly put Lawrence Knowles in a good frame of mind when he toured the Agawam Hunt in East Providence, Rhode Island, one afternoon. Now, Lawrence was not about to walk in and call it a day. He still had another nine to go, and we all know that golfers feel that their game just has to get better. For Knowles, it did. He came in with a 36. The 27-stroke difference is the largest margin of improvement for any golfer breaking 100 in a single round.

"THE MOST EXQUISITELY satisfying act in the world of golf is that of throwing a club."

—HENRY LONGHURST

"WHAT IS LOVE compared with holing out before your opponent?"

—P. G. WODEHOUSE

The 647-Yard Double-Eagle

NEITHER WIND NOR rain—nor typhoons—seem to be able to stop the appointed rounds of a golfer. Playing at the Guam Navy Golf Club on January 3, 1982, after a typhoon had just passed, Chief Petty Officer Kevin Murray had a 40-mph wind to deal with, and it certainly helped him on the 647-yard par-5. Hitting on a hard fairway with the wind at his back, his drive was later measured at 387 yards. Then Kevin took a 4-iron, which hit about 20 yards short of the green, bounced, and rolled into the cup for the longest double-eagle ever recorded.

"THE PLAYER MAY experiment about his swing, his grip, his stance. It is only when he begins asking his caddie's advice that he is getting on dangerous ground."

—SIR WALTER SIMPSON

The Trials of Golf

"Once you've had them, you've got them."

—Tommy Armour, on the yips, *"And Then Arnie Told Chi Chi . . ."*

Is That an Oil Painting?

TOMMY BOLT WAS famous for his temper on the golf course. It was sometimes volatile, other times a subtle expression of his displeasure. A famous example of the latter was the time Bolt was playing in the first round of a Tour event at the Whitemarsh Country Club in Philadelphia. On a par-3 with a two-level green and the pin cut on the back (upper) portion, Bolt hit a wonderful tee shot that landed on the lower level and jumped up to within a foot of the hole.

This brilliant display of shot-making received not a sound of recognition from the sizable gallery behind the green, a non-response that prompted Bolt to say to his caddie, "Son, I know I can't see very well anymore, but my hearing is still okay. Tell me, is that an oil painting of people behind that green?" When told it was a live audience, Bolt said, "Well, if those folks don't appreciate the shot I just hit up there, old Tom Bolt is not playing here anymore." With that, Bolt withdrew from the tournament.

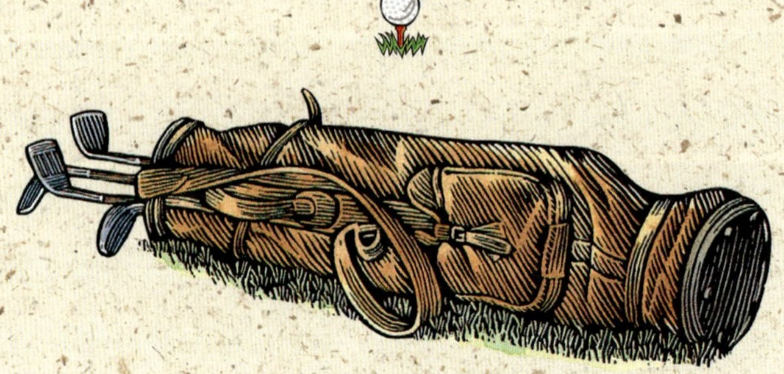

"I'M HITTING THE woods great, but I'm having trouble getting out of them."

—HARRY TOSCANO

"WHEN YOU HEAR a golfer enlarging upon the cruel ill-treatment which his ball suffered after 'one of the finest shots that was ever played,' you need not hastily conclude that the stroke was one of any really transcendent merit."

—HORACE HUTCHINSON

"NOTHING GOES DOWN slower than a golf handicap."

—BOBBY NICHOLS

"EASY. I MISSED a 20-footer for a 12."

—ARNOLD PALMER, ON HOW HE MADE A 13 ON A HOLE

The Ghost of Billy Joe Patton

IN THE 1954 Masters, North Carolinian Billy Joe Patton made a run to become the first amateur to win the prestigious title. However, he was going up against Ben Hogan and Sam Snead, and by the 12th hole of the final round he had fallen back. Thus, at the dogleg-left par-5 13th hole, Patton decided to go for the green on his second shot, hoping to make a birdie, or even an eagle. His hopes of an upset were dashed, however, when the ball ended up in the creek before the green.

Thirty years later, Ben Crenshaw led the tournament by a slender margin and faced the same choice Patton had. A student of golf history, Crenshaw knew of Patton's demise. Still, he contemplated going for the green, even after seeing Tom Kite—competing for the same title—put his tee shot in the water on the 12th. Ben gave pause before making his decision.

Crenshaw later said that he looked into the gallery for his father, hoping for a sign of what to do. Instead, however, his eye fell on a beam of sunlight filtering through the pines to spotlight Billy Joe Patton. Crenshaw had had a vision, for Patton was nowhere near the scene. Crenshaw opted not to go for it. He laid up short of the creek, then went on to win his first major title.

"Maybe I'm not adding up my scorecard right or something."

—Lee Janzen, on the fact that he felt like he was playing better but was getting worse results

"Your financial cost can best be figured when you realize that if you were to devote the same time and energy to business instead of golf, you would be a millionaire in approximately six weeks."

—Buddy Hackett

"Golf is a game whose aim is to hit a very small ball into an even smaller hole, with weapons singularly ill-designed for the purpose."

—Winston Churchill

Jack's Little Pit Stop

MOVING IN ON the leader in the 1978 U.S. Open during the third round of play, Jack Nicklaus hit a perfect tee shot on the par-4 13th hole, leaving him only 30 yards from the green. But as he walked toward his ball, there came an urgent call of nature, and Nicklaus hurried to a nearby portable toilet to seek relief. That done, he went about his other business—but not very well. He mishit his second shot into a creek fronting the green, played his fourth shot into a bunker behind the green, then took three more shots before holing out for a disastrous 7. The fiasco pretty much took him out of contention.

At his press conference following the round, Nicklaus was queried about what happened back at the 13th hole. He explained that he had to make a pit stop. In retrospect, was he sorry he did so? Did it perhaps break his playing rhythm and cost him the championship? "No," Nicklaus replied, "I had to go."

"It took me 17 years to get 3,000 hits in baseball. I did it in one afternoon on the golf course."

—Hank Aaron

"I do not remember having met any golfer who did not consider himself on the whole a remarkably unlucky one."

—Horace Hutchinson

"I can airmail the golf ball, but sometimes I don't put the right address on it."

—Jim Dent

"Pressure is playing for ten dollars when you've only got five in your pocket."

—Lee Trevino

A Third-Round Knockout

THE 11TH HOLE at the Merion Golf Club is one of the richer stretches of golf turf in the game's history—in terms of its design and historical events occurring on it. It was on the 11th where Bobby Jones closed out Eugene Homans in the final match of the 1930 U.S. Amateur to complete his fabulous Grand Slam. It was also the scene of a humorous, albeit somewhat tragic, happening that had an odd twist.

At 370 yards, the 11th is not exceptionally long. However, the green is fronted by a narrow stream known as "Baffling Brook," which also winds its way closely around the right side and rear of the putting surface. The approach is with a short iron for top players, but any approach can be unnerving. Walter Hagen once dubbed the hole "Black Friday."

Bobby Cruickshank, a Scottish pro of wide renown in the early days of American golf, was leading the field after two rounds of the 1934 U.S. Open, and he was holding on well when in the third round he came to the 11th. Here he hit a 7-iron approach that was a bit on the weak side. The ball descended into Baffling Brook, but incredibly it landed on a rock and bounced onto the green. Cruickshank was so elated by this wonderful turn of events that he threw his club high in the air and shouted, "Thank you, Lord!"

But as soon as his words left his mouth, Bobby was knocked in the head by the falling club he had tossed in glee. He was felled by the blow. His playing partner, Wiffy Cox, reacted in the guise of a boxing referee and began to count Bobby out—they had a sense of humor in those days. But Cox wasn't entirely out of order. Cruickshank was so shaken up after the incident that he finished the third round with a 77, then shot a 76 in the final round to finish two strokes off the winning pace.

"MY FAVOURITE SHOTS are the practice swing and the conceded putt."

—LORD ROBERTSON

Hole in One Not Good Enough

PLAYING AN EVENING match with Ed Winter in 1964 at Roehampton Golf Course in England, Bill Carey hit his tee shot at the 7th and felt it was pretty close to the hole. As the sun was about to set, both golfers looked for the ball in vain and kept searching as it became dark. Unable to locate it, Carey conceded the hole.

Then it dawned on him to look in the cup and, sure enough, there was his ball. He had made a hole in one—but still lost the hole.

"THE BACK IS not made to do the things we do. The only thing worse is rodeo."

—FRED COUPLES

"HEY, IS THIS room out of bounds?"

—ALEX KARRAS, AFTER HITTING A SHOT THROUGH A CLUBHOUSE WINDOW

"I MADE $3 million doing it my way and $125,000 doing it everyone else's way. I decided to go back to my way."

—HAL SUTTON, ON HIS SWING CHANGES

"IF PROFANITY HAD any influence on the flight of the ball, the game would be played far better than it is."

—HORACE HUTCHINSON

"IF YOU WATCH a game, it's fun. If you play it, it's recreation. If you work at it, it's golf."

—BOB HOPE

"GOLF IS THE hardest game in the world. There's no way you can ever get it. Just when you think you do, the game jumps up and puts you in your place."

—BEN CRENSHAW, *GOLF TALK*

David Mulligan's Do-Over

IN THE LATE 1920s, four golfers played fairly regularly at the St. Lambert Country Club near Montreal. One of the men had an automobile, and it was his job to drive to the course with the other members of the group. The route included driving over a bridge with cross ties, constructed that way to take care of horse-drawn wagons.

They would rush to the tee upon arrival, but the driver, shaken by crossing the bridge, usually hit a poor shot. Since he was the only one with an automobile, it was a common practice to allow him to hit a second tee shot. After all, they didn't want to lose their transportation. The golfer's name was David Mulligan, manager of the Windsor Hotel in Montreal, and the act of hitting a second shot off the 1st tee became known as "hitting a Mulligan."

"PLAYERS SHOULD PICK up bomb and shell splinters from the fairways in order to save damage to the mowers."

—RULE IN GREAT BRITAIN DURING WORLD WAR II

"BE FUNNY ON a golf course? Do I kid my best friend's mother about her heart condition?"

—PHIL SILVERS

"I WOULD RATHER play Hamlet with no rehearsal than golf on television."

—JACK LEMMON

"THE GAME WAS easy for me as a kid, and I had to play a while to find out how hard it is."

—RAY FLOYD

Two Strokes for Blowing the Bug

Lloyd Mangrum was only a stroke behind Ben Hogan as they prepared to putt on the 16th hole of a playoff at the 1950 U.S. Open at Merion Golf Club. On the par-4, Hogan had a six-foot putt for a birdie, and Mangrum an eight-footer for his par. As Mangrum stood over his putt, he saw a bug crawling around on the top of his ball. Inexplicably for a veteran professional who had played much golf under ultimate pressure, Mangrum picked up his ball (a clear penalty), blew the bug off it, replaced it, and proceeded to hole his putt. Hogan then missed his birdie chance, and it appeared that Mangrum had dodged the prospect of being two strokes down with only two holes to play.

However, with Mangrum about to play his tee shot on the 17th, he was stopped by Ike Grainger, the USGA official for the contest, who informed Mangrum that by picking up his ball as he did on the previous green (without marking it, although even that would have been illegal according to the rules at the time), he had incurred a two-stroke penalty. "You mean I had a 6 instead of a 4?" snarled a livid Mangrum, who with his razor-thin physique and riverboat gambler's moustache had a menacing mien. Grainger nodded yes. Mangrum was quiet for a moment, realized he had erred and said, "Well, I guess we'll all eat tomorrow."

Of course, Mangrum was now out of contention, as was George Fazio, and Hogan won the historic championship only 16 months after nearly dying from the effects of a violent highway collision between an auto and a bus. At the presentation ceremony, Mangrum did manage to salve his hurt a little when USGA President Jim Standish mistakenly referred to the Merion Golf Club by its former name, the Merion Cricket Club. Upon accepting his check for second place, Mangrum remarked, "The [USGA] brass may not know where they are, but they sure do know the rules."

"BASEBALL PLAYERS QUIT playing and they take up golf. Basketball players quit, take up golf. Football players quit, take up golf. What are we supposed to take up when we quit?"

—GEORGE ARCHER

Bad Hops

At the New Grampians Inn course in Victoria, Australia, a penalty of one stroke is added if the golfer hits a kangaroo. Apparently, there are a lot more kangaroos at the Yeppoon Golf Club in Queensland. The local rule at that course is: "A ball hitting a kangaroo—play as is."

"You can talk to a fade, but a hook won't listen."

—Lee Trevino

"In golf, I'm one under. One under a tree, one under a rock, one under a bush. . . ."

—Gerry Cheevers, former NHL goalie

"Nobody wins the U.S. Open. It wins you."

—Cary Middlecoff

"IF I SWUNG a gavel the way I swung that golf club, the nation would be in a helluva mess."

—TIP O'NEILL, FORMER SPEAKER OF THE HOUSE

"IT IS A law of nature that everybody plays a hole badly when going through."

—BERNARD DARWIN, *PLAYING THE LIKE*

"MY BEST SCORE ever is 103. But I've only been playing 15 years."

—ALEX KARRAS

"GOLF IS A game where guts, stick-to-it-iveness, and blind devotion will get you nothing but an ulcer."

—TOMMY BOLT

The Big Picture

"Golf is like a love affair. If you don't take it seriously, it's not fun. If you take it too seriously, it breaks your heart."

—Arnold Daly

A Whole Different Ballgame

Baseball's Ted Williams and golf's Sam Snead once got into a discussion about which game was harder to play. Williams took the lead, pointing out that in golf the ball isn't moving and you hit it off a flat surface. In baseball, he said, "I gotta stand up there with a round bat and hit a ball that's traveling at me at around a hundred miles an hour, and curving."

Snead considered that for a moment, then responded: "Yeah, Ted, but you don't have to go up in the stands and play your foul balls. Golfers do."

"If it weren't for golf, I'd probably be a caddie today."

—George Archer

"Golf is a bloodless sport—if you don't count ulcers."

—Dick Schaap, *Massacre at Winged Foot*

"UNLIKE THE OTHER Scottish game of whisky-drinking, excess in golf is not injurious to the health."

—SIR WALTER SIMPSON

"I NEVER PRAY on the golf course. Actually, the Lord answers my prayers everywhere except on the course."

—REV. BILLY GRAHAM

"THE ONLY WAY of really finding out a man's true character is to play golf with him."

—P. G. WODEHOUSE

"THREE THINGS ARE as unfathomable as they are fascinating to the masculine mind: metaphysics, golf, and the feminine heart."

—ARNOLD HAULTAIN

Penick's Precocious Pupil

HARVEY PENICK, THE legendary Texas teaching professional whose most famous students included Tom Kite, Ben Crenshaw, and Mickey Wright, was reminiscing once about an experience with Crenshaw. He recalled the time Crenshaw's father brought his eight-year-old son to Penick for his first lessons. Using a 7-iron cut down to size, Crenshaw was asked to hit some balls to a green about 75 yards away.

Little Ben did just that, and was then told to go up there and putt the ball into the hole. Ben said, "If you wanted it in the hole, why didn't you tell me in the first place?"

"I GUESS THERE is nothing that will get your mind off everything like golf. I have never been depressed enough to take up the game, but they say you get so sore at yourself you forget to hate your enemies."

—WILL ROGERS

"Golf is a compromise between what your ego wants you to do, what experience tells you to do, and what your nerves will let you do."

—Bruce Crampton

"The difference between now and when I played during my younger days is my drives are shorter and my short game is longer."

—Simon Hobday

"Golf appeals to the idiot in us and the child. Just how childlike golf players become is proven by their frequent inability to count past five."

—John Updike

No Time to Govern

According to some reports, President Dwight Eisenhower made 29 trips to Augusta National Golf Club while in office. Another calculation was made that he played 800 rounds of golf during the eight years of his presidency, 221 of them at Augusta. It seems that the estimates are a bit high, because that would have been one round every four days, a big number even for a retiree.

Still, there were a number of Americans who felt Ike spent too much time on the golf course. A bumper sticker that popped up during his time in the White House read: "Ben Hogan for President. If we're going to have a golfer, let's have a good one."

"Regarding the practice of no other sport perhaps on the face of the earth is there so much difference of opinion as in that of golf. The confusion and multiplicity of styles that prevail among players are proof enough of this."

—H. B. Farnie

Mrs. Hogan's Advice

ONCE HE CONQUERED the tendency to hook the ball badly with his driver, Ben Hogan became one of golf's most accurate shot-makers both from the tee and with his approach shots. He got even better in this part of the game after a word of advice from his wife, Valerie.

Ben was at best a moderately good putter and eventually a very poor one. At one point in the middle of his competitive career, Hogan was going through a particularly bad stretch of putting and was complaining regularly about it to his wife, reiterating that he couldn't make a thing from outside 20 feet. At that, Valerie told her husband, "Then hit the ball closer to the hole."

"GOLFERS AS A rule are an exceptionally honest race of men, but uncertain arithmetic is occasionally encountered on the green."

—HENRY E. HOWLAND

Keep Your Chin Up

JACK BURKE, JR., winner of 17 PGA Tour events, including a PGA Championship and a Masters title during the 1950s, was the son of a pioneering golf teacher who regularly entertained at his dinner table the likes of Ben Hogan, Jimmy Demaret, and other greats of their era. The conversation was almost always about golf—swing technique and how to teach it, how to play shots, and so forth. Young Burke was a good listener, and as he matured he put much of what he had heard from the best of players and teachers into his own game and teaching of golf.

However, Burke had a rather unique way of expressing himself. For example, in order to avoid swinging across the ball from outside to inside the target line, Burke declared that the "inside of the ball belongs to you." This is to say, concentrate on hitting the left-rear "corner" of the ball to keep from cutting across it and slicing. He also once recalled being told that animals with lowered heads get eaten. "Pigs and cows get eaten, leopards don't. Leopards have their heads up. You never saw Hogan with his head down. Nicklaus never has his head down. They walk in a room and they're looking. Like good boxers. Losers have their heads down; winners have their heads up."

"There is no shape nor size of body, no awkwardness nor ungainliness, which puts good golf beyond reach."

—Sir Walter Simpson

"I'd give up golf if I didn't have so many sweaters."

—Bob Hope

"There are three ways of learning golf: by study, which is the most wearisome; by imitation, which is the most fallacious; and by experience, which is the most bitter."

—Robert Browning

Wethered and the Rumbling Train

Bobby Jones once said that Joyce Wethered was the best golfer, man or woman, he had ever seen.

Wethered, who was at her peak in the 1920s and '30s, had a classic golf swing that was the envy of one and all. But she also had the capacity for concentration that is as much the mark of a great champion as swing technique. Wethered exhibited this side of her talent in her very first tournament. As an unknown 19-year-old, Wethered made it to the finals of the 1920 Women's English Championship and faced the reigning queen of British golf, Cecil Leitch. A railway line ran close to the 17th green of the course, and it was there where Wethered began to make her reputation.

Four down after the first 18 holes, Wethered fought her way back, and when she reached the 17th (35th) hole she was one up on Leitch. On the green, she had a short putt that, if she made it, would close out the match. As she stood over the ball about ready to begin her stroke, a train thundered past on the nearby track. Wethered, however, without a pause and with the train still rumbling by, calmly stroked her ball into the hole to win the title. When asked later why she hadn't waited until the train had passed before playing, Wethered said, with some surprise, "What train?"

"THE GAME IS one of the most exasperating hitherto devised by the wit of man."

—H.S.C. EVERARD

"GIVE ME A man with big hands and big feet and no brains and I'll make a golfer out of him."

—WALTER HAGEN

"MY SOLE AMBITION in the game is to do well enough to give it up."

—DAVID FEHERTY

The Ibaraki Country Club Scam

Golfers waiting for their starting time at a public course have been known to grumble because there were too many golfers. Even the private club member gets upset when calling for a Saturday morning time only to find that the earliest he can get off the 1st tee is noon.

Take heart: It could be a lot worse. Consider that the typical golf club in Japan might have 2,800 members. Next, take the case of Ken Mizuno. In February 1992, he was arrested by Japanese authorities on charges of evading $44.4 million in taxes. It seems that Mr. Mizuno, who has no connection with the golf and sports equipment manufacturer, sold some memberships to Japanese residents so they could tee it up at Ibaraki Country Club northeast of Tokyo. Mizuno sold memberships at anywhere between $13,950 and $54,260, and he wasn't satisfied selling just 2,800. He sold 52,000 memberships to the club. Now that could make for a long wait on the 1st tee.

"Golf is not a funeral, though both can be very sad affairs."

—Bernard Darwin

"I'M GOING TO have a lot of college to pay for, so I'm definitely going to try to play the Senior Tour."

—HOWARD TWITTY, FATHER OF SIX

"I'M ONLY SCARED of three things: lightning, a sidehill putt, and Ben Hogan."

—SAM SNEAD

"A GOLFER RARELY needs to hit a spectacular shot unless the one that precedes it was pretty bad."

—HARVEY PENICK, *AND IF YOU PLAY GOLF, YOU'RE MY FRIEND*

"EIGHTEEN HOLES OF match or medal play will tell you more about your foe than will 18 years of dealing with him across a desk."

—GRANTLAND RICE

Don't Bet on It

A STATISTICAL STUDY taken in 1980 came up with the following odds on making a hole in one: 3,708-to-1 for a male professional or expert amateur; 4,658-to-1 for a female professional or talented amateur; and for the average golfer, it was 42,952-to-1. An update of that study was developed in 1987 by *Golf Digest.* Using statistics from their Hole-in-One Clearing House, the magazine determined that on any one hole, the odds were still the same for a male or female professional, but they were 33,676-to-1 for the average golfer. The average golfer apparently either got better or luckier in those seven years.

"GOLF IS THE only game in the world in which a precise knowledge of the rules can earn one a reputation for bad sportsmanship."

—PATRICK CAMPBELL, *HOW TO BECOME A SCRATCH GOLFER*

"GOLF IS THE hardest game in the world to play and the easiest to cheat at."

—DAVE HILL

"THE DIFFERENCE BETWEEN golf and government is that in golf you can't improve your lie."

—GEORGE DEUKMEJIAN, FORMER GOVERNOR OF CALIFORNIA

"IF YOU PICK up a golfer and hold it close to your ear, like a conch shell, and listen, you will hear an alibi."

—FRED BECK

"THINKING MUST BE the hardest thing to do in golf, because we do so little of it."

—HARVEY PENICK

Cuff That Cheater

Frank Beard once wrote that everyone cheats when they first start playing golf, and some never stop. It seems like a little thing, because golfers insist that if you cheat, you're only cheating yourself. That may be, but a few golfers who played in a charity event thought that enough was enough.

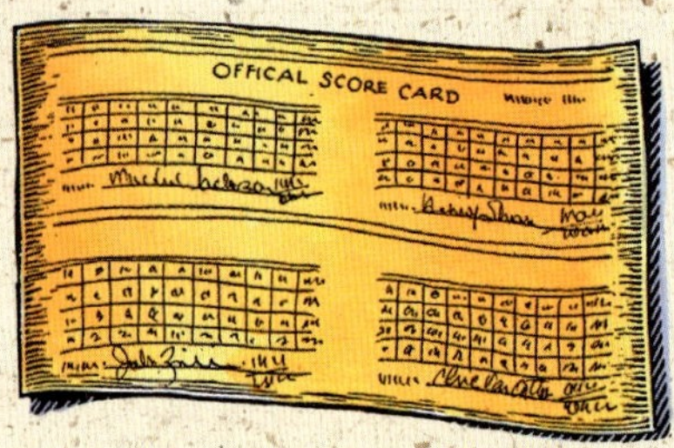

Charles Carey, of Indiana, had a reputation of lowering his score, according to some who played with him. In one tournament, director Scott Montross was asked to have a bit of surveillance done on Carey's game. Hired detectives kept a safe distance from him and observed his round through binoculars. Carey turned in a score of 67, which the detectives said was at least 13 strokes lower than his actual score.

Carey was arrested by police for altering his score in the 1993 American Diabetes Association fundraiser, charging him with theft for trying to collect a $50 gift certificate. It might have been the first incident where a golfer was arrested for cheating.

Interactive Television

GOLFERS CAN ALWAYS use a break, especially if the opponent is Byron Nelson and the course is Pine Valley. From 1962 to 1970, *Shell's Wonderful World of Golf* was a popular telecast, pitting some of the legends of the game against each other on the greatest golf courses in the world. The first to be filmed was Byron Nelson, then age 49, against Gene Littler, the U.S. Open champion. It wasn't the first matchup shown on the program, but it was the first to be filmed.

There weren't a great many camera operators in 1961 who had experience in televising a golf event. Rounding up seven cameras to cover the match was even a bigger chore. The competition was at stroke play, not at match, so a big number on any hole could spell defeat. No other course could offer more possibilities of a big number than Pine Valley, either.

Littler, known as "Gene the Machine" for his silky smooth swing, was normally a very straight driver, but not on this occasion. His tee shot on the 1st hole hooked into the woods. One of the camera operators, who was not a golfer, picked up the ball, threw it back to Gene, and said, "Do it over. I missed it." Littler still lost to Nelson by two strokes.

Bipartisan Politics

BEING INVITED TO the White House is something most people would greatly welcome. It has become a tradition for the President of the United States to invite championship teams from various sports to the White House. Most have graciously accepted the invitation, regardless of who was in office or the political leanings of the invitees.

President Clinton made an offer to the 1993 U.S. Ryder Cup team to visit him in the Rose Garden before they made their way to The Belfry in England. Some members were quite outspoken, stating that they would pass up the invitation because of differences they had with the President's policies. Cooler heads prevailed, and the team did show up for their meeting. Captain Tom Watson, a liberal turned conservative, showed his diplomacy when, after presenting the President with a staff bag and sweatshirt, said, "The golf grip is like politics. If you turn too far right, you always get in trouble from the left. The obvious place is to grip it somewhere so you can place it down the middle." All was forgiven.

"GOLF SWINGS ARE like snowflakes. There are no two exactly alike."

—PETER JACOBSEN, *BURIED LIES*

"GOLF TOURNAMENTS ARE lonely. In baseball there's eight other guys to keep me company."

—WALTER HAGEN, WHEN ASKED WHY HE PREFERRED BASEBALL TO GOLF

"THE BIGGEST LIAR in the world is the golfer who claims he plays the game merely for exercise."

—TOMMY BOLT, *GOLF: A GOOD WALK SPOILED*

"GOLF IS A game where you yell 'fore,' shoot 6, and write down 5."

—PAUL HARVEY, *GOLF DIGEST*

The Players

"He is the boldest of all players. The game has never seen one like him. The epitaph on his tombstone ought to read: 'Here lies Arnold Palmer. He went for the green.'"

—MARK MCCORMACK, *ARNIE: THE EVOLUTION OF A LEGEND*

The Name's Heafner, Not Heefner

IN THE EARLY days of the PGA Tour, when the purses were very small and only the first 16 places shared the scant offerings, players doing poorly and who had little chance of picking up a check were more likely to withdraw in mid-tournament. They could save on expenses by getting out of town. Also, because of the minimal purses, players seemed to feel a need to maintain their sense of self-esteem and would withdraw if hurting either physically or psychologically. Some of those withdrawals had bizarre twists.

Ky Laffoon once withdrew from a Western Open because the players' parking lot was too far from the clubhouse. At a Houston Open plagued by steady rains, Tommy Bolt stood in the middle of the 5th fairway during his third round waiting to play his approach. Disgruntled and uncomfortable, the always nattily attired pro said, "I'm wearing a cashmere sweater worth a hundred dollars, shoes worth a hundred and a half, slacks worth 75. Hell, I'm ruining clothes worth more than I can win. I'm leaving."

Clayton Heafner, a huge and gruff man whom Jimmy Demaret once described as having a very even temperament—"he's mad all the time"—was not introduced on the 1st tee at the start of the first round of an Oakland Open as he would have liked. He was announced as Clayton Heefner from Linville, North Carolina, who hopefully would not have the same trouble with the trees that he had the previous year in the tournament. Heafner's face crunched up in beet-red anger. He then stood over the trembling announcer and said, "My name is not Heefner; it's Heafner [as in 'Heff-ner']. I'm from Charlotte, not Linville, and I'm not going to give myself the chance to get into your damn trees again." He told his caddie to put his clubs in his car, and ten minutes later he drove off.

In another tournament, Heafner's opening drive was a poor snap-hook into trees on the left. He told his caddie to go get the ball; he was withdrawing. A woman in the gallery heard this and confronted Heafner, telling him he couldn't quit because she had him in a calcutta pool. "Well, all right," said Heafner, who then turned to his caddie. "Leave the ball." Then he departed the premises.

"I never wanted to be a millionaire. I just wanted to live like one."

—Walter Hagen

Wright Grades a D

Before embarking on a successful career as a professional golfer, which included 82 victories, Mickey Wright was a student at Stanford. Mickey was arguably the finest female golfer of all time. An authority no less than Ben Hogan said that she possibly had the best swing in the history of the game, man or woman.

One of the classes Wright took while in college was golf, and her final grade was a D. Admitting to being a bit of a smart aleck, Mickey said she probably deserved the low mark she was given by a Mrs. Brown.

"I don't like No. 4 balls. And I don't like 5s, 6s, or 7s on my scorecard."

—George Archer, on his superstitions

"Tommy Bolt's putter has more air time than Lindbergh."

—Jimmy Demaret

"When I want to really blast one, I just loosen my girdle and let 'er fly."

—Babe Zaharias, *Story of American Golf*

"The professional, as we are now chiefly acquainted with him, is a feckless, reckless creature. In the golfing season in Scotland he makes his money all the day, and spends it all the night. His sole loves are golf and whiskey."

—Horace Hutchinson

Tight Security

During the 1926 British Open, Bobby Jones forgot the badge that enabled him to enter the grounds so he could compete. He tried to get through the gate, but an official turned him away. Jones simply went to the public entrance and bought a ticket. Of course, he won the championship.

The Headbanger

Ivan Gantz had no success as a Tour player in the 1950s, but he became kind of an underground legend in the game because of his outrageous temper. His most bizarre act of anger was to whack himself in the head with his putter after missing a crucial putt.

"Actually, that happened a few times," Gantz once recalled. "I was playing on the Tour in Houston, at Memorial Park, and missed a short putt on the last green that would have given me a 68. Man, I raised that putter up and knocked myself in the head with it. I made a pretty good chunk in there, but I didn't fall down and I wasn't knocked cold, like a lot of people said. People exaggerate."

"I don't know if I'll be allowed to play the Senior Tour anymore. My knee's only a few months old, my back is 17 years old, and I recently got a new hip. I might be too young now."

—George Archer

"LIKE THE CLASSIC plays and symphonies, Sam Snead doesn't belong to just one generation. His mark will be left on golf for eternity."

—PETER THOMSON

"THE ONLY REASON I played golf was so I could afford to hunt and fish."

—SAM SNEAD

"WATSON WALKS ABOUT his golf course business like a young trial lawyer going from one courtroom to the next."

—AL BARKOW, *GOLF'S GOLDEN GRIND*

"THE PRESSURE MAKES me more intent about each shot. Pressure on the last few holes makes me play better."

—NANCY LOPEZ, *GOLF'S MENTAL MAGIC*

Laffoon's Buffoonery

One of the most colorful characters in American golf in the early days of the PGA Tour was Ky Laffoon, who displayed fine skills but a mercurial temperament. He won 12 times on the Tour, with 1934 his best season. That year, he won the Park Hill Open in Denver with the lowest 72-hole score on a regulation course recorded up to that time (266), and he took the Eastern Open by eight shots. In the Western Open, Laffoon shot all six rounds (including two in a playoff) in the 60s while losing to Harry Cooper. In 1934, he was the first golfer ever to record a stroke average for the year below 70 (69.1).

But Laffoon would be best remembered for his temper, which sometimes reached absurd proportions. The most legendary example was the time he putted poorly in a tournament, tied his putter to the bumper of his car, and dragged it 1,000 miles across Texas "to make that sumbitch pay for betraying me."

Another time, after going through a poor stretch of golf, he vowed he would never again take more than 72 strokes in a tournament round. Never! The following week, in Sacramento, he shot rounds of 67, 69, and 65 and had a fine chance to win. However, in the last round he came to the 18th hole with a six-foot putt for a birdie. He missed the putt, then picked up his ball, put it in his pocket, and walked away without finishing the hole. In doing so, he effectively disqualified himself. When asked why he did what he did, Laffoon explained that the six-foot putt would have given him a 72. The next one, of course, would have given him a 73, and by not putting out he made good on his pledge.

"OLD TOM IS the most remote point to which we can carry back our genealogical inquiries into the golfing style, so that we may virtually accept him as the common golfing ancestor who has stamped the features of his style most distinctly on his descendants."

—HORACE HUTCHINSON, ON OLD TOM MORRIS

"GREG IS ONE of the classiest ever to play this game. That's why he's so popular with all the other players, even when he beats us."

—PETER JACOBSEN, ON GREG NORMAN, *GAME DAY*

Sarazen's Sand Blaster

GENE SARAZEN WAS one of the greatest golfers in the game's history, but he didn't stand on his talent for shot-making alone. He was always looking for innovations in equipment that would help make him a champion. To improve his grip, he adopted and popularized the "Reminder Grip," with its flat front surface on which the left thumb could fit more comfortably. But his most striking innovation was his design of the first legal sand wedge, which was a revolutionary development in equipment.

The golfers of Sarazen's era, even the best of them, were generally poor players from greenside bunkers because they had to use a niblick (9-iron) with a sharp leading edge that dug too deeply in the sand. To mitigate the problem, Sarazen in 1932 conceived the idea of building a flange on the back of a niblick that was angled so the rear portion of it hit the sand before the leading edge. One could now hit behind the ball without fear of digging too deeply. The ball would be exploded out on the force of the flying sand.

After weeks of experimenting with his new club, Sarazen realized he had something special. "It got so I would bet even money I could go down in two out of the sand," he once recalled. That year, he took his wedge with him to play in the British Open. During the practice rounds, he amazed everyone with his ability to play from the bunkers, and many people wondered about the "new weapon" Sarazen had in his bag. But Sarazen knew better than to brandish the club for all to see, in particular the officials running the honorable championship.

"After every practice round, I put the club under my coat and took it back to the hotel with me," Sarazen recounted, "because if the British had seen it before the tournament began, they would have barred it. Oh, yes. Once the tournament was underway, they couldn't do that. I went down in two from most of the bunkers." And he won the championship.

"You can start your soft-boiled eggs by the time he's ready."

—Johnny Miller, on Nick Faldo's slow play

"If Tommy Bolt had a head on his shoulders, he would have been the best golfer who ever lived."

—Ben Hogan

Short Arms and Deep Pockets

A FAMILIAR SIGHT on the practice greens at the PGA Tour sites years ago was a man named George Low. He was the self-proclaimed best putter in the world. His one claim to fame on Tour happened in 1945 when he took the first-place check at the New Orleans Open. He didn't win the tournament. Freddie Haas did, but Freddie was an amateur so George got the money. It brought Byron Nelson's all-time record streak of 11 straight victories to an end.

The other professionals called Low "America's Guest." Without question, George was tighter with a buck than Sam Snead. He once was an assistant pro to Vic Ghezzi in Deal, New Jersey. One of Low's favorite tricks was to solder a dime to the head of a nail and pound it into the floor of the pro shop. Then he would stand in the corner, watching members practically break their fingernails when they tried to pick up the coin.

"HE PLAYS A game with which I'm not familiar."

—BOBBY JONES, ON JACK NICKLAUS

"He hits the ball nine million miles and without a swing that looks like he's trying to."

—Jack Nicklaus, on Tiger Woods

"All my life I've wanted to play golf like Jack Nicklaus, and now I do."

—Paul Harvey, after Nicklaus shot an 83 in a tournament

"I know I got drunk last night, but how did I wind up at Squaw Valley?"

—Jimmy Demaret, on waking up to see Pebble Beach covered with snow

"It's a shame, but he'll never make a golfer—too much temper."

—Alex Smith, golf professional, on Bobby Jones

The Tale of Wiffi's Hat

When Wiffi Smith arrived on the golf scene, some stated she was the next Babe Zaharias. She just might have been if a wrist injury hadn't cut short a fine but brief LPGA career. Smith was a free spirit, driving a Model A from tournament to tournament and hitting drives with great authority. Freckle-faced Wiffi was an all-American girl, with maybe a bit of tomboy thrown in. In short, she was delightful.

Her last year as an amateur was 1956. It was a good one, as she was named to the Curtis Cup team and captured the British Amateur and French Amateur.

Following her win in the British Amateur, Wiffi was invited to a garden party at Buckingham Palace, where she was to meet Queen Elizabeth II. She was given instructions on the proper protocol and also informed that the occasion called for her to wear a hat. Outside of wearing a visor once or twice, Wiffi had never owned a hat. She was taken to Harrods, where she found one, not necessarily to her liking but less offensive than others she tried.

When the time arrived, Wiffi took a taxi to Buckingham Palace, sure that everyone was looking at her and the silly hat. She met the queen, performing the proper curtsy, then mingled with the other guests. When the first opportunity presented itself, she went to the ladies' room, removed the hat, and left it there. She was about to leave when a female employee came running after her and presented Wiffi with the hat she had "accidentally" left behind. Wiffi thanked her and gave her a tip.

Smith jumped in the taxi, returning to the hotel. During the ride, she stuffed the hat under the seat in front. After paying the driver, she went to the room. A few minutes later, there was a knock on the door. It was the cab driver, hat in hand, delivering the unwanted item that was "accidentally" left behind. Wiffi thanked the driver and tipped him for his trouble. The next morning, she packed, called for a bellhop, and left the hat in the room. As she was getting into the taxi to take her to the ship she was catching for France, an out-of-breath hotel employee rushed up and presented her with the hat that he knew she had "accidentally" left in the room. Wiffi thanked and tipped him. By this time, she had given more in tips than the hat had cost originally.

Wiffi did not leave the hat in the cab, having learned her lesson on the way to the hotel. The last time she saw the hat was when she threw it overboard somewhere in the English Channel.

Snead vs. Hogan

Sam Snead and Ben Hogan were archrivals during their heydays. And, at least for Hogan, even representing their country as teammates was no reason to back off from the battle. Case in point: the 1956 Canada (now World) Cup Matches, played at the Wentworth Golf Club outside London, England.

Snead had been playing unevenly, but after two rounds he was still in contention for the individual title. Hogan was leading. They drove together to the course, and going out for the third round Snead complained about how poorly he was playing. Hogan said, "Sam, I can tell you one thing to do that will make you unbeatable." Snead was all ears. "What's that?" he asked. "Not now," Hogan said. "I'll tell you later."

That day, Hogan shot a course-record 67 that for all intents and purposes locked up the individual title. He was now ready to "help" his teammate. The next morning, he told Snead that by pointing his left toe a bit more toward the target at address, he would make a freer and fuller swing. Snead went out and shot his best round of the week, a 68 (which Hogan matched). Asked if Hogan's tip was responsible for his fine round, Snead said, "Hell, no! I hit the shots." A tale of two egos.

"At my best, I never came close to the golf Byron Nelson shoots."

—Bobby Jones

"On being asked how good Young Tom Morris really was, an aged golfer replied: 'I cannot imagine anyone playing better.'"

—Anonymous

Chi Chi's Superstitions

Are golfers superstitious? Most are, although few will admit it. Take Chi Chi Rodriguez, for example. He said he marks his birdie putts with a quarter but switches to a buffalo nickel for pars and eagles. If the quarter isn't working, Chi Chi has been known to change to a gold piece for birdies. Rodriguez said that no matter which coin he uses, he always places it with heads showing, not tails. One other thing: Chi Chi won't ever use a ball with a number higher than 4.

The Courses

"Pebble Beach and Cypress Point make you want to play. Spyglass Hill—that's different; that makes you want to go fishing."

—JACK NICKLAUS, *THE GREATEST GAME OF ALL*

Steam Shovel Charley

CHARLES HENRY BANKS was a popular golf course designer in the 1930s who was noted for the enormously high walls of his greenside bunkers and severe undulations in his greens. He made extensive use of the steam shovel, which had come to the fore in course building around his time.

Indeed, Banks came to be nicknamed "Steam Shovel Charley," especially after a bizarre incident while Banks was remodeling the Whippoorwill Club course in Armonk, New York. There had been heavy rains, and Banks's steam shovel sank in some especially soft ground around the 6th fairway, the operator barely escaping before the machine slipped under. Legend has it that the steam shovel is still there, beneath a pond.

"THE REASON THE Road Hole is the greatest par-4 in the world is because it's a par-5."

—BEN CRENSHAW, ON THE 17TH HOLE AT ST. ANDREWS

"You can play a damned good shot and find the ball in a damned bad place."

—George Duncan, on St. Andrews

"There's nothing wrong with St. Andrews that 100 bulldozers couldn't put right. The Old Course needs a dry clean and press."

—Ed Furgol

"Harbour Town is so tough, even your clubs get tired."

—Charles Price, *Inside Golf*

"Modern architects could take a great lesson by looking at this course."

—Billy Casper, on Merion, *The U.S. Open*

The Perfect Golf Course

GOLF ARCHITECT PETE Dye was once asked what constituted a "great" golf course. His response cut to the heart of so-called greatness, and it reflected a touch of cynicism. "A great championship golf course," said Dye, "has the Atlantic Ocean on one side, the Pacific Ocean on the other, and Arnold Palmer winning a tournament on it."

"THE COURSE IS playing the players instead of the players playing the course."

—WALTER HAGEN, ON THE 1951 U.S. OPEN AT OAKLAND HILLS

"THERE ARE 118 golf holes here. All I have to do is eliminate the 100."

—ARCHITECT PERRY MAXWELL, ON HIS PRAIRIE DUNES COURSE, *1993 GOLF ALMANAC*

"WE DON'T WANT to get anybody killed. Of course, if we could pick which ones, it might be a different story."

—HORD HARDIN, AUGUSTA NATIONAL CHAIRMAN, ANNOUNCING THAT PLAY IN THE 1983 MASTERS WOULD BE POSTPONED DUE TO LIGHTNING

"I'VE GOT A lawnmower back in Texas. I'll send it over."

—BEN HOGAN, AT THE 1953 BRITISH OPEN AT CARNOUSTIE

"YOU WOULD LIKE to gather up several holes from Prestwick and mail them to your top 10 enemies."

—DAN JENKINS

"GETTING IN A water hazard is like being in a plane crash—the result is final. Landing in a bunker is similar to an automobile accident—there is a chance of recovery."

—BOBBY JONES, *THE ANATOMY OF A GOLF COURSE*

The Course Record

It began in 1919. Up to that time, Ralph Kennedy had played on 176 different golf courses and had signed scorecards to prove it. He hadn't intended to save them as proof; it was simply a way of remembering the game he loved so much.

Kennedy met Charles Leonard Fletcher, a Briton claiming to have played 240 courses, which he felt was a world record. He also had the scorecards to authenticate the accomplishment. Looking at that as a challenge, by 1926 Kennedy had matched Fletcher's total, which then stood at 445. He wasn't done.

When Ralph turned 50 in 1932, he reached the 1,000-course milestone. Still, he kept the cards, which were mostly signed by the golf professionals at the sites he had played, and they were carefully placed in a safe-deposit box.

The big day came on September 17, 1951. Kennedy placed his ball on the 1st tee of the Old Course at St. Andrews. All of the golf he had played didn't help him overcome the jitters he felt as he prepared to hit the drive on his 3,000th course. Fortunately, Ralph hit the ball 180 yards right down the middle of the fairway. By the end of his career, Kennedy had played on 3,035 different courses, which remains the official record.

High Standards in Singapore

DURING A BUSINESS trip to Asia, Bob McMasters and Marty Koss decided to see if they could get a round of golf in while they were in Singapore. They called the Sembawang Country Club and were told they could have a starting time the following morning at eight o'clock. Bob was then asked if he had a handicap card. Bob assured the lady that they had handicaps but didn't bring their cards with them. He informed her that he was a 3 while Marty was a 12.

It seems that the club had a rule that if you did not have your card with you, it was necessary to take a performance test prior to being allowed on the course. They arrived at the course about an hour early and made their way to the practice range, where they were each required to purchase a bucket of balls. Now, here was Bob, who had been good enough to have won his club championship and qualify for six different USGA national championships, taking a proficiency test. He grabbed a 1-iron, rifled two shots directly over the 200-meter marker, and the assistant professional said, "Leave the rest of the balls there." Marty had to work a bit harder, hitting three 9-irons before he was given the same instructions.

Ho-Hum, a Hole in One

Laurence Curtis was introduced to golf in 1892, and he was so taken by it that he convinced the executive committee of his club, The Country Club in Brookline, Massachusetts, that a course be built for the members. A six-hole course was built, and it opened in April 1893 with an exhibition played by Curtis, Arthur Hunnewell, and George Cabot.

When Hunnewell made a 90-yard hole in one, the gallery hardly responded at all. They reasoned that, being an expert at the game, Hunnewell had simply done what was expected. In fact, when none of the other players holed in one as did Hunnewell, the galleryites walked off convinced that the game would not become very popular.

"Golf architecture is an art closely allied to that of the artist or sculptor, but also necessitating a scientific knowledge of many other subjects."

—Alister Mackenzie

"AUGUSTA IS ONE type of course and I'm another type of golfer."

—LEE TREVINO, *THEY CALL ME SUPER MEX*

"IT'S LIKE PLAYING basketball against Patrick Ewing. There's never a safe shot."

—TOM WATSON, ON THE BAY HILL COURSE, *1993 GOLF ALMANAC*

"PUTTING GREENS ARE to golf courses what faces are to portraits."

—CHARLES B. MACDONALD, *THE ANATOMY OF A GOLF COURSE*

"I'VE ALWAYS SAID that if they have a golf course like this in heaven, I want to be the head pro."

—GARY PLAYER, ON AUGUSTA NATIONAL

A Roundabout Bogey

During the 1970 British Open at St. Andrews, Tommy Shaw seemed to have no problem on the 1st hole with a nice drive and an approach that found the green. That the ball came to rest above the hole didn't present too much of a problem for a professional of his talent. After all, he had successfully negotiated a number of fast greens on the PGA Tour.

His putt was a bit strong, as Shaw was envisioning a birdie start, and he was a little surprised as he watched the ball gain speed, rolling off the green and coming to rest in the Swilcan Burn. Undaunted, he dropped a ball on the other side and hit a wedge into the hole for a slightly unorthodox bogey. He went down in history as one of the rare golfers to hit a green in regulation in the British Open, make only one putt, and still end up 1-over-par for the hole.

"Hazeltine is a mean old golf course."

—Lee Trevino, *They Call Me Super Mex*

"GOLF ARCHITECTS CAN'T play golf themselves and make damn sure no one else can."

—ANONYMOUS

"THIS COURSE IS 90 percent horse manure and 10 percent luck."

—J. C. SNEAD, ON THE TPC AT SAWGRASS, *BURY ME IN A POT BUNKER*

"THE GREATEST COMPLIMENT that can be paid to the architect is for players to think his artificial work is natural."

—ALISTER MACKENZIE

"IT'S STAR WARS golf. The place was designed by Darth Vader."

—BEN CRENSHAW, ON THE TOURNAMENT PLAYERS CLUB AT SAWGRASS, *BURY ME IN A POT BUNKER*

You Were Saying?

PRIOR TO THE 1954 U.S. Open, Robert Trent Jones was called upon to redesign some of the holes at Baltusrol's Lower Course. He had done the same thing at Oakland Hills prior to the '51 Open, a course that Ben Hogan had called "The Monster" while others had used unprintable terms. Naturally, there were some concerns about how difficult Jones would make the course, not to mention the criticism from members who weren't trying to win a major, just enjoy a round of golf.

The one hole that caused a great deal of comment was the 4th, an innocent par-3 until the architect got through with it. After the modification, the shot had to carry some 190 yards over water from the championship tee to reach the green. Even host professional Johnny Farrell criticized the design and difficulty of the hole. Farrell wasn't just any club professional; he had been one of the headliners during the 1920s.

Trent visited the club, listening to the concerns and comments. Finally, he sent Frank Duane, his design associate, to fetch a club and ball. The three went to the 4th hole, where Jones teed up, swung the iron, and watched as the ball went into the cup for an ace. End of discussion.

"I'M GLAD I brought this course, this monster, to its knees."

—BEN HOGAN, AFTER HIS 1951 U.S. OPEN WIN AT OAKLAND HILLS

"YOU NEED A doctorate degree to putt at Augusta National."

—JOHNNY MILLER

"PAR IS WHATEVER I say it is. I've got one hole that's a par-23, and yesterday I damn near birdied the sucker."

—WILLIE NELSON, ON THE COURSE HE BUILT HIMSELF

"TROUBLE ONCE BEGUN at this hole may never come to an end till the card is torn into a thousand fragments."

—BERNARD DARWIN, ON THE 11TH AT ST. ANDREWS

Professional Advice

"He wanted me to change my takeaway, my backswing, my downswing, and my follow-through. He said I could still play right-handed."

—Brad Bryant, on receiving instruction from David Leadbetter

Shoot the Lowest Score

In 1994, Nick Faldo had a chance to meet the reclusive, famously terse Ben Hogan for the first time. Faldo had by now won the Masters twice and the British Open three times, but he had yet to capture a U.S. Open. During his meeting with Hogan, he thought he might get a clue about that—some psychological or strategic insight to how he could win. Hogan had a history of careful and thoughtful preparation for the U.S. Open. He had won it four times and finished second twice.

Thus, it was not unreasonable for Faldo to ask, "How do you win the U.S. Open?" Hogan looked across his desk with his steely blue eyes fixed on Faldo and responded, "Shoot the lowest score." Faldo thought he was kidding, although there was not a trace of humor in the answer. Still, he asked again. "No really, Mr. Hogan, how do you win the U.S. Open?" Hogan sat upright in his chair, leaned toward the young Briton, and this time gave him the notorious Hogan glare as he repeated his original answer: "Shoot the lowest score." With that, Hogan turned away. The interview was over. Faldo, baffled, rose and left shaking his head.

The advice, of course, was absolutely correct. It just didn't have any frills. Hogan was not one for frills.

"You've just got one problem. You stand too close to the ball—after you've hit it."

—Sam Snead

"Always throw clubs ahead of you. That way, you don't have to waste energy going back to pick them up."

—Tommy Bolt

"He told me just to keep the ball low."

—Chi Chi Rodriguez, on the advice his caddie gave on a putt

"One very simple tip will infinitely improve the timing of most golfers. Merely pause briefly at the top of the backswing."

—Tommy Armour, *How to Play Your Best Golf All the Time*

Get a Little Closer

ONCE, WHILE GIVING a clinic to a group of college golfers, Byron Nelson was asked, "How close can you, or should you, stand to the ball at address?" Nelson replied, "Son, you can't stand too close to the ball." Jack Nicklaus would say essentially the same thing when asked the question. "I've seen a lot of amateur golfers move farther away from the ball at address," Nicklaus said, "but I've never seen one move closer to it."

"THE CARDINAL ERROR which players commit today when they practice is to nudge each shot onto a perfect lie."

—GENE SARAZEN, *THE COMPLETE GOLFER*

"THAT'S A BAGFUL of indecision."

—JACKIE BURKE, WHEN ARNOLD PALMER BROUGHT EIGHT PUTTERS TO THE PRACTICE GREEN

"FRANCIS, BE SURE to keep your eye on the ball."

—10-YEAR-OLD CADDIE EDDIE LOWERY'S ADVICE TO FRANCIS OUIMET ON THE FIRST TEE OF AN 18-HOLE PLAYOFF FOR THE 1913 U.S. OPEN

"IF YOU WERE asked to imagine what flavor of ice cream would describe your golf swing, I would like to hear you answer 'vanilla.'"

HARVEY PENICK, *AND IF YOU PLAY GOLF, YOU'RE MY FRIEND*

"THROUGH YEARS OF experience, I have found that air offers less resistance than dirt."

—JACK NICKLAUS, ON WHY HE TEES THE BALL HIGH

Practice Your Bad Lies

GENE SARAZEN WAS walking along a practice range where a number of golfers were hitting balls. "Look at 'em," said Sarazen, in one of his more acerbic moods. "Every one of those golfers is taking perfect lies for every shot. They're making it too easy for themselves. The practice isn't worth the time they're spending at it. You know how many of those good lies you get on a golf course? If they really want a good practice, if they really want to learn how to play golf, they should be hitting balls out of long grass—and divots."

"IN PLAYING A single, the novice should neither select for his antagonist one very much worse or very much better than himself."

—H. B. FARNIE

"THE GOOD GOLFER feels his swing as all one piece."

—PERCY BOOMER, *THE COMPLETE GOLFER*

"GOOD PUTTING STARTS with seeing the ball going into the hole before you take your stance—in fact, before you even take your putter in hand."

—DAVE STOCKTON, *DAVE STOCKTON'S PUTT TO WIN*

"IF A LOT of people gripped a knife and fork the way they do a golf club, they'd starve to death."

—SAM SNEAD

"A CARDINAL RULE for the club breaker is never to break your putter and driver in the same match or you are dead."

—TOMMY BOLT, *HOW TO KEEP YOUR TEMPER ON THE GOLF COURSE*

"I DON'T TRUST doctors. They are like golfers. Every one has a different answer to your problem."

—SEVE BALLESTEROS, *SEVE: THE YOUNG CHAMPION*

Hold Her Gently

THERE HAVE BEEN many metaphors for how gently a golf club should be held, how light the pressure should be on the handle. For example, you should hold it as if it were an overripe tomato or a balloon you don't want to pop. But Jimmy Demaret had the most memorable: "Hold the club as though it were the girl you want to marry."

"IF YOU FIND your adversary complaining to an intolerable degree of your good luck and his own bad, it is a satisfaction to bear in mind that, though you have no remedy in the present, in the future you have a very adequate one—never to play with him again."

—HORACE HUTCHINSON

The Slow-Motion Approach

TOMMY BOLT WAS acknowledged by all of his contemporaries as one of the finest shot-makers in golf, an artist who could skillfully manipulate the golf ball for distance and trajectory as the situation required. At the same time, Bolt was not one to indulge in swing theory. Instead, he played by feel.

For instance, during the playing of a Pro-Am one day on the Senior Tour, Bolt hit a 7-iron approach from about 135 yards, a distance he could easily have covered with a 9-iron. When asked by one of his amateur partners why he used the longer club, Bolt said he wanted to hit the ball lower because of the wind in his face, and because the pin was at the back part of the green and a 7-iron shot was more likely to land and run back to it. When the amateur then asked Bolt how he hit such a shot, he said, ingeniously, "Oh, you just slow down your arms."

"IT IS IMPOSSIBLE to outplay an opponent you cannot out-think."

—LAWSON LITTLE

A Little More to the Right

Walter Hagen, for all his outstanding achievements as a championship golfer, was not inclined to theorize a great deal, if at all, about the mechanics of the golf swing. Indeed, his swing was in general quite rambunctious—it has been generously characterized as a controlled lunge. His swing, and how he went about his golf, matched his personality and the way he lived his life off the golf course—improvisationally. He could be a very wild driver of the ball but had a marvelous gift for recovery shots from difficult places, and he had as deft a touch with the putter as the game has ever seen.

It was often the latter that pulled Hagen through. Thus, he devised a "philosophy" for playing the game from the tee to green. If on the practice tee before a round, or even early in the round itself, he found himself hitting the ball from right to left—hooking it—on that day he simply aimed a little more to the right to allow for the hook. If the next day he found himself hitting the ball from left to right—cutting or even slicing it—he aimed more to the left. Simple as that.

"READING A GREEN is like reading the small type of a contract. If you don't read it with painstaking care, you are likely to be in trouble."

—CLAUDE HARMON

"THERE IS ONE essential only in the golf swing: The ball must be hit."

—SIR WALTER SIMPSON

"IT'S GOOD SPORTSMANSHIP not to pick up lost golf balls while they are still rolling."

—MARK TWAIN

"THE MAIN THING for the novice or the average golfer is to keep any conscious hand action out of his swing."

—BEN HOGAN, *FIVE LESSONS: THE MODERN FUNDAMENTALS OF GOLF*

Hagen's Helpful Tips

Sam Snead had entered the 1946 British Open primarily at the urging of his manager, Fred Corcoran. The day before he planned to leave, Sam told Corcoran he wouldn't be going. It was during the Inverness Four-Ball in Toledo, Ohio, and Snead explained that he just wasn't putting well enough.

Fred mentioned this to Walter Hagen, who was at the tournament. The Haig felt Sam could handle the greens at St. Andrews and that it was the duty of American pros to try to win the British Open. After Sam finished his round, Hagen escorted him to the locker room. In a far corner, Hagen asked Snead to hit some putts. After watching a few strokes, he gave some advice to The Slammer, and soon Sam was hitting the putts crisply, dead to target. Sam told his manager he would make the trip after all, so Corcoran informed the press about the incident.

The next day, the local paper carried a story on the first sports page headlined "Snead to Play in British Open—Takes

Putting Lesson from Walter Hagen." Sam was writing a syndicated column at the time, and on the same page was that column with another headline: "How to Putt by Sam Snead." Snead won the British Open that year with some deft putting.

"KEEP ON HITTING it straight until the wee ball goes into the hole."

—JAMES BRAID

"I'M A POSITIVE thinker. My dad would kill me if I wasn't."

—PGA TOUR PLAYER DAVE STOCKTON, JR.

"LOOKING UP IS the biggest alibi ever invented to explain a terrible shot. By the time you look up, you've already made the mistake that caused the bad shot."

—HARVEY PENICK, *THE BEST OF HARVEY PENICK'S LITTLE RED BOOK*

Two Strokes for Sharing

PAIRED WITH LEE Trevino during the final round of the 1980 Tournament of Champions at La Costa Resort, Tom Watson was cruising through his round as they approached the next tee. Lee was not on his game. Instead of his normal fade, shots were going left on the Merry Mex. On the other hand, Tom was continuing his torrid pace, about to win his third tournament of the season.

Wanting to help his friend, Watson told Lee he was playing the ball too far forward in his stance. The comment went out over national television, and a viewer called La Costa. By the time Tom got to the scorer's tent, PGA Tour director Jack Tuthill caught up with him, making an inquiry as to the incident. Watson readily admitted he had given advice and was promptly assessed a two-stroke penalty. Had Tom signed the card before the discussion with Tuthill, he could have been disqualified. He still won the tournament by three strokes, but there was a piece of irony connected to the incident: Watson had just authored a book on the rules of golf for the USGA.

"HIT IT A bloody sight 'arder, mate."

—ENGLISH PRO TED RAY, WHEN ASKED HOW TO DRIVE THE BALL FARTHER

"NOTHING IS MORE important than swinging the club at a pace you can comfortably control."

—NICK FALDO, *FALDO: A SWING FOR THE AGES*

"A GOLFER'S SWING is often made for good or bad in the first week of his experience."

—HARRY VARDON

"THERE ARE NO secrets to golf. The secret of success is practice, constant but intelligent practice."

—ERNEST JONES, *AT RANDOM THROUGH THE GREEN*

Abusive Advice

ONE OF THE many players given the designation "The Finest Golfer to Have Never Won a Major" was Archie Compston, a good British professional. In addition to having won several tournaments in Europe, Compston is best remembered for an exhibition match with Walter Hagen that was scheduled to be played over 72 holes. It didn't last that long, however. Hagen was not in very good form, having not played golf for quite some time, and requested a delay. It was denied, and Walter received the worst defeat of his career, 18 & 17. Compston was immediately picked as the favorite to win the British Open. When it was over, The Haig was the champion.

After his competitive days were over, Compston became the professional at Mid-Ocean, an exclusive club in Bermuda and a favorite of both Americans and Britons wanting to enjoy the wonders the island had to offer. As with many professionals who had attained a degree of success as tournament players, Compston was not the most patient of teachers. He expected students, both beginners and those more accomplished, to be able to hit shots the way he could. Naturally, it never worked that way or the pupils wouldn't have come to him for lessons in the first place.

One day he was instructing a titled British woman who had just taken up the game. She was not used to the verbal abuse she was receiving from Archie. After one tongue-lashing, she swung the club directly at the pro, hitting him solidly on his shin. Grabbing his leg and jumping on one foot, Compston exclaimed, "That's the swing! Now hit the ball the same way."

"It will take three fine shots to get there in two, sir."

—Scottish caddie

"When they start hitting back, it's time to quit."

—Henry Ransom, when his shot from the beach at Cypress Point rebounded off a rock and hit him in the stomach

"I probably spend more time fine-tuning the quality of my grip and set-up position than I do checking anything else."

—Nick Faldo, *Faldo: A Swing for the Ages*

The Mental Game

"Oh, hang it! With so many things to be thought of all at once, steady play is impossible."

—Sir Walter Simpson

Stone Age Wisdom

The noted sports psychologist Bob Rotella was once asked to talk about the "yips," that malady of maladies among golfers that affects putting more than anything else, especially short pressure putts. The gist of his remarks revolved around an evolutionary phenomenon called the fight-or-flight syndrome.

To wit, back in the Stone Age, if not before, people had only sticks and stones to defend themselves, and when they went forth to fetch food, they would often run into voracious wild animals bent on making the people their meal. At this, people responded with fear, which triggered a physical reaction. Blood moved to fill the deeper and larger muscles, so if they chose to either fight the enemy or run from the enemy, the people would be stronger where they needed to be.

Although people have long since developed weapons to defend themselves in such situations, the effects of the syndrome have not yet disappeared. Thus, when faced with a tough, downhill right-to-left four-footer to save par and win the club championship, a number of things occur physically that work against us. For instance, blood is diverted from a number of places, such as the stomach, which is why we feel a hollowness there when facing a touchy putt. Blood also leaves the fingers, making them less sensitive. Hence, the most important part of a golfer's physique under the circumstances is desensitized, and the stroke is less likely to be smooth and controlled.

Until such time as we shuck off fight-or-flight syndrome, what is a golfer with the yips to do? Rotella suggests shaking your hands vigorously between shots to get some blood back in the fingers. Also, hormones secreted from the brain in a stressful situation cause constriction of the muscles around the chest and throat. Hence, the feeling of "choking" is based in reality. So, take a lot of deep breaths when under the gun.

One of Gene Sarazen's favorite dicta was "miss 'em quick," which can be applied to the yips. "The longer you stand there, the harder the putt gets," said Sarazen. Tommy Bolt expanded on that by saying, "The longer you take to hit a putt, the more you think of ways to miss it."

In short, you can't take flight from the pressure situation, but you can fight it.

If You Talk the Talk . . .

SETTING UP THE pairings for the first two rounds can be an art, especially in the major championships. It's not unusual to have past champions together, so it came as a bit of a surprise when Ian Baker-Finch complained that he was being paired with some has-been at the 1995 British Open. That has-been was Arnold Palmer, making his farewell visit to St. Andrews at the oldest of golf championships.

Baker-Finch was announced and took his place on the 1st tee. The wind was up, which seems to be the case more often than not at St. Andrews, and as he was swinging, his visor blew off. Ian half-heartedly completed the swing with disastrous results. He smothered the drive, which barely got off the ground. The ball started left and continued until it crossed the 18th fairway, finally finishing on the road out of bounds. Even a whiff would have produced better results.

While always the gentleman, it was difficult for Arnold to hide the smile on his face after observing what might have been the worst drive ever hit on the 1st tee of a British Open by a past champion.

"I TRY TO use a method I call the positive-negative approach. I positively identify the negatives and work from there."

—BOB MURPHY

"THERE ARE TWO kinds of golf—golf and tournament golf. They are not the same."

—BOBBY JONES

"MANY GOLFERS HAVE a habit of observing, before playing, that they have a very bad lie, so as to discount, to themselves and others, the discredit of their prospective miss."

—HORACE HUTCHINSON

"THE PERSON I fear most in the last two rounds is myself."

—TOM WATSON

Psyche Analysis

With his book *The Mystery of Golf*, published in 1908, Canadian writer Arnold Haultain became effectively golf's first sports psychologist. No one before him had ever dissected and articulated the mental side of golf, and all who today make this their profession have a copy of his book on their shelf. If they don't, they should, lest they think they are conjuring original ideas. Here is a brief example of Haultain on why golf is, as the saying goes, 80 percent mental... at least:

"Golf, indeed, is a fruitful field of psychological phenomena. For example, hypnotists of the most modern school aver, I believe, that there exist somewhere in the brain or mind of man five distinct layers of consciousness. For proofs of multiple consciousness the hypnotist should frequent the links. He will there often find one layer of consciousness roundly upbraiding another, sometimes in the most violent language of abuse, for a foozled stroke; and so earnest sometimes is the vituperation poured by the unmerciful abuser upon the unfortunate foozler, that truly one is apt sometimes sincerely to commiserate with the former, and to regard him as the victim of a multiple personality, and not at all blameable for his own poor play.

Golfers, too, have I known who imagine themselves constantly accompanied by a sort of Socratic daimon prompting them to this, that, or the other method of manipulating the club—without doubt a mystic manner of looking upon one's alter ego. It would be interesting to 'suggest' to a duffer, while in the cataleptic trance, to keep his eye on the ball, and to follow through, and then to watch the result. If these fundamental rules (so easy to preach, so difficult to practice) could be relegated to some automatic sub-stratum of consciousness, leaving the higher centres free to judge of distance and direction (for it is thus, probably, that the man who has golfed from childhood plays), the task of many a professional might be simplified. All of which goes to show that, in the game of golf, the mind plays a larger part than, in many quarters, is apt to be imagined."

"A CONSERVATIVE STRATEGY joined to a cocky swing produces low scores. Reckless boldness joined to a doubtful swing is a formula for disaster."

—DR. BOB ROTELLA, *GOLF IS A GAME OF CONFIDENCE*

13 Strokes of Bad Luck

In 1977, Tsuneyuki Nakajima became the youngest Japanese PGA champion in history. He was rewarded with an invitation to play in the Masters the following year. Nakajima eventually became known to golfing fans around the world as "Tommy," although he was still Tsuneyuki when he made his first trip to Augusta.

He was even-par on Friday as he came to the Azalea Hole. Unfortunately, he had scored an 80 in his opening round. In order to make the cut, Tommy was going to have to make a few birdies, so maybe an eagle here would make his task a bit easier. Trying to hit a long drive, Nakajima hooked it into the water, took a drop, and hit his next shot only about 90 yards. Then he hit his fourth in the creek in front of the green.

Thinking he might be able to hit out of the water, Tommy took a swing and the ball came down on top of his shoe. That resulted in a two-stroke penalty. Now the total was seven. Handing the club back to his caddie so it could be cleaned caused another two-stroke penalty when it was dropped in the hazard. He was successful on the next swing, although the ball went over the green. From there in, it was routine—a chip and two putts for a 13, thus breaking the record high in the Masters for one hole, set by Frank Walsh in 1935 when he scored a 12 on the 8th.

The press asked Tommy to come to the interview room and, being a gentleman, he agreed. When asked if he lost his concentration, he replied through an interpreter, "No, I lost count."

"While, on the whole, playing through the green is the part of the game most trying to the temper, putting is the most trying to the nerves."

—A. J. Balfour

"If you hear a man complaining of having 'lost all interest' in a match which he has lately played, you will be pretty safe in inferring that he lost it."

—Horace Hutchinson

"Golf is a fickle game, and must be wooed to be won."

—Willie Park, Jr.

The Kid's Got Nerve

Remembered mostly for the way he dressed on the course, Doug Sanders was not a fashion plate when he grew up in Cedartown, Georgia. Instead, he was like many of the teenagers of the day, wearing jeans and a T-shirt.

When only 13, Doug went to Augusta to play in the Georgia State Junior. He carried his own bag and certainly gave no indication of the kind of life he would one day live on the PGA Tour. For his first-round opponent he drew a local lad, dressed to the nines who had his own caddie. Not wanting to have any disadvantage in the match and, in fact, hoping to turn the odds in his favor, Doug teed up his ball, turned to the boy, and said, "I'm Sanders from Cedartown. I'll play you five, five, and five."

Here he was: 13 years old, playing in a state tournament, and willing to bet money on the outcome. His opponent was so rattled that he could hardly get the tee in the ground and was never a factor in the match.

"GOLF HAS DRAWBACKS. It is possible, by too much of it, to destroy the mind."

—SIR WALTER SIMPSON

"GOLF IS A day spent in a round of strenuous idleness."

—WILLIAM WORDSWORTH

"A SECRET DISBELIEF in the enemy's play is very useful for match play."

—SIR WALTER SIMPSON

"SHOW ME A golfer who walks away calmly after topping a drive or missing a kick-in putt, and I'll show you one who is going to lose."

—SAM SNEAD, *AT RANDOM THROUGH THE GREEN*

Tossin' and Turnin'

Leo Diegel was a brilliant golfer who had the misfortune of being in his prime during the era when Walter Hagen was at his peak and golf's dominant player. What's more, Diegel had a famously nervous disposition. Hagen, the master competitor, knew of this, and while attending an all-night party on the eve of his final-round match with Diegel for the 1926 PGA Championship, Hagen was told that his opponent for the next day was already in bed. Hagen replied, "Yes, but he isn't sleeping." Hagen won, 5 & 3.

"Action before thought is the ruination of most of your shots."

—Tommy Armour, *How to Play Your Best Golf All the Time*

"If you lose your temper, you will most likely lose the match."

—Horace Hutchinson

"THE LEAST THING upset him on the links. He missed short putts because of the uproar of butterflies in the adjoining meadows."

—P. G. WODEHOUSE, "ORDEAL BY GOLF"

"EXCESSIVE GOLFING DWARFS the intellect. Nor is this to be wondered at when we consider that the more fatuously vacant the mind is, the better for play."

—SIR WALTER SIMPSON

Japanese Taboos

IF YOU'RE PLAYING golf in Japan, chances are pretty good you won't run into someone using a golf ball with the number 4 on it. That's a bad-luck number for the Japanese, and they do not manufacture any for the locals. Instead, a dozen Japanese balls are numbered 1, 2, 3, and 7.

Tunnel Vision

THE YEAR BEFORE Claude Harmon won the Masters, he was paired with Ben Hogan in that spring classic. Bantam Ben was known for his powers of concentration, and an incident on the 12th probably is a great example of that virtue that all golfers would like to have.

Harmon hit his tee shot into the cup for an ace, and the large gallery cheered, yelled, and applauded for a considerable period of time. Hogan said nothing but waited until the noise had subsided, then hit his shot on the green. When they got on the putting surface, Claude walked over to the hole and picked the ball out of the cup, at which time there was more thunderous applause. He acknowledged the cheers as Hogan read his line, but still Ben did not say a word. Hogan then struck the putt, which went into the hole for a 2, and there was more applause.

As they reached the 13th tee, Hogan turned to Harmon and said, "That's the first birdie I've had on that hole in three years." He was so wrapped up in his own game, it never occurred to Ben to congratulate Claude on his hole in one.

"THE WORST CLUB in my bag is my brain."

—CHRIS PERRY

"IN ALMOST ALL other games, you pit yourself against a mortal foe; in golf, it is yourself against the world."

—ARNOLD HAULTAIN

"THE MAJORITY TREAT the hole as a place more difficult to get into than it really is."

—SIR WALTER SIMPSON

"NEARLY ALL GOLFERS would be better off if they forgot about the score as they played."

—DR. BOB ROTELLA, *GOLF IS A GAME OF CONFIDENCE*

Aoki's Fortune Cookie

DURING THE EVENING before the final round of the 1983 Buick Open, Japanese professional Isao Aoki decided to have Chinese food for dinner. When he finished the meal, he opened his fortune cookie, which had a message that read, "You will take a trip to the desert." Sure enough, the next day Isao twice hit bunkers that resulted in bogeys, and he lost the tournament by one stroke.

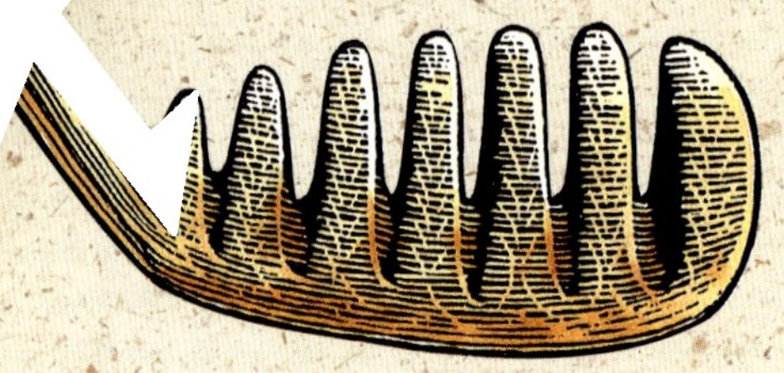

"GIVEN AN EQUALITY of strength and skill, the victory in golf will be to him who is captain of his soul."

—ARNOLD HAULTAIN

"IT IS NOTHING new or original to say that golf is played one stroke at a time. But it took me many years to realize it."

—BOBBY JONES

"THOSE WHO CANNOT drive suppose themselves to be good putters."

—SIR WALTER SIMPSON

"PEOPLE TAKE FOR granted that we're all mental giants. But it takes time to develop the correct frame of mind."

—PAUL AZINGER

Death of a Putter

FORMER BRITISH OPEN champion Kel Nagle didn't have one of his better days in the final round of the 1978 New Zealand Open. After posting an 82, he went over to the club's flagpole and lowered the flag to half-staff. "That is in memory of my putter," he said, "which has died."

Wisecracks

"If I had to choose between my wife and my putter, well, I'd miss her."

—Gary Player

Faldo, King of the Jungle

Nick Faldo belied his perceived stoic and humorless personality during the second round of the 1992 U.S. Open at the Pebble Beach Golf Links. At the par-5 14th hole, Faldo hit his third shot into a tree beside the green. He and everyone else saw the ball go into the tree, but no one saw it come down. Faldo decided to climb the tree to look for his ball, for if he found it he could declare it unplayable and incur only a one-stroke penalty, rather than a two-stroke penalty for a lost ball.

He climbed partway up the tree and shook it. Nothing fell. The gallery called out for him to go higher. Faldo did, shook the branches again . . . but to no avail. At this point, with the gallery laughing, Faldo rose to the occasion. Thinking of himself as Tarzan swinging on a jungle liana, he shouted as loudly as he could, "Where the hell is Jane?"

"My handicap? Woods and irons."

—Chris Codiroli, former major-league pitcher

"THE HARDEST SHOT is a mashie at 90 yards from the green, where the ball has to be played against an oak tree, bounced back into a sand trap, hits a stone, bounces on the green, and then rolls into the cup. That shot is so difficult, I have only made it once."

—ZEPPO MARX

"I KNOW I'M getting better at golf because I'm hitting fewer spectators."

—GERALD FORD

"GEORGE, YOU LOOK perfect—that beautiful knitted shirt, an alpaca sweater, those expensive slacks. You've got an alligator bag, the finest matched irons, and the best woods money can buy. It's a damned shame you have to spoil it by playing golf."

—LLOYD MANGRUM, TO COMEDIAN GEORGE BURNS

Blame It on the Caddie

LEE TREVINO CAME to the 72nd hole of the 1971 U.S. Open, at the Merion Golf Club outside Philadelphia, knowing he was in a fight to the finish with Jack Nicklaus, who was playing in a pairing just behind. The 18th tee at Merion is a smallish area set on a rise near a fence. The gallery in this cramped area was packed tight. Trevino had a difficult time getting through it to reach the tee.

In the heat of the moment, he was ready and anxious to play his drive on the par-4 hole. He spit into the glove on his left hand and went to the edge of the tee to get his driver. But his bag wasn't there, for his caddie was having even more trouble getting through the crowd and hadn't reached it by the time Trevino was ready to play. Trevino's eyes opened wide in surprise at this break in his rhythm. The crowd was hushed in the tension of the moment.

Then Trevino broke the strain he and everyone else was feeling by saying, "I'm doing the playing, and my caddie's choking!" The crowd roared with relieved laughter, as did Trevino, who went on to defeat Nicklaus in a playoff the next day for the championship.

"If he takes the option of dropping behind the point where the ball entered the hazard, his nearest drop is Honolulu."

—Jimmy Demaret, on a penalty faced by Arnold Palmer at Pebble Beach

"Your clubs."

—Jackie Gleason, when asked by Toots Shor what to give the caddie after shooting 211

"Give me golf clubs, the fresh air, and a beautiful partner, and you can keep the golf clubs and the fresh air."

—Jack Benny

"Never bet with anyone you meet on the 1st tee who has a deep suntan, a 1-iron in his bag, and squinty eyes."

—Dave Marr

What a Dump!

In 1946, Sam Snead was talked into entering the British Open, being played on the famed Old Course at St. Andrews. Snead had never played in the championship, and this was his first visit to Scotland. While driving along the periphery of the course on his way to his hotel, Snead looked over and saw the hallowed ground. His reaction was rather sacrilegious (although he didn't know it at that moment) when he said to his friend and manager, Fred Corcoran, "Freddie, that looks like an old, abandoned golf course." Be that as it may, Snead won the championship.

"If you drink, don't drive. Don't even putt."

—Dean Martin

"I don't care to join any club that's prepared to have me as a member."

—Groucho Marx

"When he gets the ball into a tough place, that's when he's most relaxed. I think it's because he has so much experience at it."

—Don Christopher, Jack Lemmon's caddie

"Obviously the deer on the fairway has seen you tee off before and knows that the safest place to be when you play is right down the middle."

—Jackie Gleason, to writer Milton Gross

"I had some uphill putts—after each of my downhill putts."

—Homero Blancas

"A lot more people beat me now."

—Dwight Eisenhower, on how his game changed after his presidency

Yo, Buddy, Move It!

BERNARD DARWIN, THE preeminent British golf writer, was, like most golfers, not very fond of slowpokes on the course. Though he was normally the quintessential British gentleman under even the most trying of such circumstances, Darwin's limit was reached one day while playing with a golfer who was especially "deliberate," as the euphemism goes for those who dawdle endlessly over their ball. After 11 holes of waiting and waiting for the fellow to begin his swing for every shot, Darwin finally said, "Sir, whatever else you may die of, it won't be from a stroke!"

"CADDIES ARE A breed of their own. If you shoot 66, they say, 'Man, we shot 66!' But go out and shoot 77 and they say, 'Hell, he shot 77!'"

—LEE TREVINO

"There are two things that won't last long in this world, and that's dogs chasing cars and pros putting for pars."

—Lee Trevino

"I was three over—one over a house, one over the patio, and one over a swimming pool."

—George Brett

"I saw a course you'd really like, Trent. On the 1st tee, you take a penalty drop."

—Jimmy Demaret, to course architect Robert Trent Jones

"My butterflies are still going strong. I just hope they are flying in formation."

—Larry Mize

No Women Allowed

IT TOOK A long time, but the main clubhouse facilities were opened to women by the Royal and Ancient Golf Club of St. Andrews for the British Ladies' Championship in 1975. The old regulation barring women had stood for 220 years.

Keith Mackenzie, the secretary of the R & A, was fond of telling the story of the British Ladies' Championship being played on the Old Course one year. The rain was coming down in torrents, but play continued. Some of the officials huddled close to the clubhouse with umbrellas open, trying to stay as dry as possible. Finally, Mackenzie walked out and the women were elated, thinking the walls were about to fall and they would be invited inside the clubhouse. Instead, they heard Keith ask, "Would you please not stand in front of the windows? You are blocking the view of the members."

"I HAVE A furniture problem. My chest has fallen into my drawers."

—BILLY CASPER

"IT WASN'T MY fault. Blame the guys in the foursome in front of me."

—PRO FOOTBALL PLAYER LAWRENCE TAYLOR, ON BEING LATE FOR PRACTICE

"NO, SIR. WE couldn't 'ave a coincidence like that."

—SCOTTISH CADDIE, ON BEING TOLD HE WAS THE WORST CADDIE IN THE WORLD

"MADAM, MODERATION IS essential in all things, but I have never failed to beat a teetotaler."

—HARRY VARDON

Are You Jimmy Demaret?

What's My Line? was a popular television show in the 1950s. Each week, there would be a mystery contestant who was generally a well-known celebrity. The four panelists were blindfolded for that portion of the show and had to guess who it was by asking questions about the guest until the guest answered no. Each time a panelist received such an answer, $5 was added to the pot for the contestant. The celebrities received money just for being on the show, although the main reason they appeared was to receive national publicity.

Jimmy Demaret was invited to be on the show, with the very first question coming from Dorothy Kilgallen. She surprised everyone by immediately asking, "Are you Jimmy Demaret?" No money was won, and the segment was much shorter than anticipated. John Daly, the host, had to fill some time. Daly asked her how she was able to come up with such an amazing guess. She explained that as she was coming up to the studio in the elevator, a handsome gentleman turned to her and introduced himself saying, "Hello, I'm Jimmy Demaret. Are you here for *What's My Line?*, too?"

"I DON'T LIKE to watch golf on television. I can't stand whispering."

—DAVID BRENNER

"GIMME: AN AGREEMENT between two losers who can't putt."

—JIM BISHOP

"I OWE EVERYTHING to golf. Where else could a guy with an IQ like mine make this much money?"

—HUBERT GREEN

"IF THE FOLLOWING foursome is pressing you, wave them through and then speed up."

—DEANE BEMAN

Wisequack

AT TIMES THERE is a great problem with Canada geese at the Oakmont Country Club in Santa Rosa, California. Anyone who has played on a course that has some of the birds can attest to the fact that they can be very messy as well as bold.

Charles Schulz was a frequent player at Oakmont. Of course, he is famous for the *Peanuts* comic strip and all of the items associated with the popular feature. An avid golfer, Schulz used the game as a subject many times. He also used animals such as Snoopy and Woodstock in his strips, so seeing geese on the course probably made him feel right at home.

In 1992, he was playing with Dean James, the head pro at Oakmont, when he spied a number of the honkers down the 8th fairway. Schulz hit a good shot that, after about three bounces, hit one of the geese. It didn't hurt the bird, who sort of jumped up and then settled down to feed again, but it might have caused the artist to lose a couple of yards. Schulz turned to James and said, "I knew I should have yelled 'quack.'"

"I'll take a two-shot penalty, but I'll be damned if I'm going to play the ball where it lies."

—Elaine Johnson, after her ball hit a tree and bounced back into her bra

"The old one didn't float too well."

—Craig Stadler, on why he was using a new putter

Shut Up, Already!

Wendy Egan, of Canberra, Australia, had a career round, shooting a 35 for the nine holes. She insisted on giving a shot-by-shot description of the round—not once, but with regularity. Her exasperated husband finally ran an ad in the personal section of the *Canberra Times* that read: "My wife played her best round of golf last Tuesday. Would those who have not yet heard about it please phone 731103 for full details of every shot... Noel Egan." The first call came at 7:00 A.M. on Saturday, and they continued all weekend.

Fast Facts

King James II of Scotland banned golf in 1457 because golfers spent too much time playing golf instead of working on their archery skills.

The $1 Million Hole in One

NOVEMBER 1, 1992, will be a date fondly remembered by Jason Bohn, a sophomore at the University of Alabama. He played in a charity event sponsored by the Golfers' Association of Alabama and made a hole in one at a 135-yarder when he was one of 12 finalists to get one shot at an ace.

It was worth $50,000 a year for 20 years. That's a cool $1 million. Of course, Jason had to forfeit his amateur status if he accepted the $1 million. It didn't take him very long to make a decision. He called his father after the great shot and said, "I have some good news and some bad news. The bad news is I'm no longer on the golf team. The good news is I'm now the fourth-highest money-winner on the PGA Tour."

THE FIRST GOLF resorts in the United States were The Homestead in Hot Springs, Virginia, and The Greenbrier in White Sulphur Springs, West Virginia. The hotels' first courses were constructed in the 1890s.

THE FIRST GOLF course ever constructed in the United States was Oakhurst Links Golf Club in White Sulphur Springs, West Virginia, in 1884. It no longer exists.

THE ONLY GOLFER to win the U.S. Open, British Open, and Canadian Open in the same year was Lee Trevino in 1971. He did it during a 21-day period.

IN THE 1930s, the USGA created a limit of 14 clubs in a bag to make the game more competitive for poorer golfers. Before then, wealthier golfers would put as many as 30 clubs in their bags.

THE FIRST GOLF balls were made of wood. The next were leather balls filled with goose feathers, followed by rubber balls, gutta-percha balls, and then modern wound balls.

The $50 Million Shot

In 1987 in Benin, West Africa, a factory overseer, Mathieu Boya, decided to spend his lunch break practicing his shot-making. The improvised range was an area adjacent to the country's main air base. One errant shot sliced over the fence, hitting a bird and knocking it onto the windshield of a jet in the process of taking off. While the pilot tried to gain control of the plane, he had little luck and it crashed into four other jets that were parked on the runway. In effect, it destroyed Benin's entire air force.

The police arrested Mr. Boya, presenting him with a bill for about $50 million, give or take a few million. He was charged with "hooliganism" and was sent to prison.

The first major championship winner was Willie Park, Sr., the winner of the 1860 British Open. He won four British Opens in his career.

Founded in 1766, Royal Blackheath Golf Club, southeast of London, was the first golf course in England. Golf had been played in Scotland for at least three centuries before.

With eight victories in the Greater Greensboro Open, Sam Snead holds the record for dominating a single PGA Tour event.

In France, Germany, and Sweden, golfers must have a license like Americans must have to hunt or fish.

The only golfers to successfully defend a Masters title were Jack Nicklaus in 1966, Nick Faldo in 1990, and Tiger Woods in 2002.

Four Aces in Four Days

SCOTT PALMER BEGAN a streak on the 260-yard par-4 6th hole at Balboa Park Municipal Course in San Diego on October 9, 1983, by holing a driver for a double-eagle and, of course, a hole in one. The next day, he recorded another ace on the 198-yard 8th with a 5-iron. Still in the groove, Scott used a wedge to get still another on the 150-yard 1st, then made it four in four days when he scored a hole in one on the 8th, this time with a 6-iron. It's the most aces made on consecutive days on record, and makes you wonder if he was a distant relative of Arnold.

THE LAST AMATEUR to win the U.S. Open was Johnny Goodman in 1933. Amateur Jack Nicklaus finished second in 1960.

THE ROYAL AND Ancient Golf Club of St. Andrews governs golf in all countries of the world except the United States.

IN 1927, 15-YEAR-OLD Byron Nelson beat 15-year-old Ben Hogan in a playoff at the Fort Worth Glen Garden Country Club Caddie Tournament.

THE FIRST SUDDEN-DEATH playoff in a major championship was the 1979 Masters, when Fuzzy Zoeller beat Tom Watson and Ed Sneed.

LEE ELDER WAS the first black golfer to play in the Masters. He qualified by winning the 1974 Monsanto (Pensacola) Open.

BETH DANIEL IS the oldest winner on the LPGA Tour. She was 46 years, eight months, and 29 days old when she won the 2003 BMO Financial Group Canadian Women's Open.

Club on Wheels

A GOLF CLUB was organized in 1982 called the Burbank Country Club. It lacked only two things—a clubhouse and a golf course.

The 50 members purchased a bus and equipped it with card tables, easy chairs, and a bar. In total, it comfortably held 28 people, and if an event had more entrants, they had to use their own transportation to get to a golf course. The club members arranged for starting times at various courses in the area and left the driving to the bus driver, at least until they got to the 1st tee.

THE ROYAL CALCUTTA Golf Club in India was the first golf course ever constructed outside the British Isles. It was constructed in 1829 by British Army officers.

IN MATCH PLAY, a golfer is "dormie" when his or her hole lead is the same as the number of holes left to play.

THE MOST SUCCESSFUL defending champion in professional golf is Walter Hagen, who won the PGA Championship four times from 1924 to 1927.

MOST GOLF COURSES in Japan have two putting greens on every hole—a bent-grass green for summer play and a korai-grass green for winter play.

FOUR GOLFERS—WILLIE ANDERSON, Ben Hogan, Jack Nicklaus, and Bobby Jones—have won the most individual career U.S. Opens: four times each.

TIGER WOODS HAS won eight PGA Player of the Year Awards (as of the 2006 season), the most won by any PGA Tour player. Tom Watson is second with six awards.

Balancing Balls

Golfers don't have to be on the course to set records. Mark Baumann of Grand Island, Nebraska, set a record of sorts when he balanced five golf balls on top of each other in 1975. The record was later tied by Robert Boyle from Regina, Saskatchewan, in 1982. Both golfers might have helped their games a little more if they had spent that time on the practice putting green.

Metal woods, very popular today, were first developed in 1896 by William Mills for the Standard Golf Company of Sunderland, England.

The longest sudden-death playoff in PGA Tour history was an 11-hole playoff between Cary Middlecoff and Lloyd Mangrum in the 1949 Motor City Open. They were declared cowinners.

THE YOUNGEST PLAYER ever to win a major championship was Young Tom Morris, who was 17 years old when he won the 1868 British Open.

GOLF WAS INTRODUCED to Ireland in the 19th century by British military occupiers.

ROCKY THOMPSON PLAYED more than 600 regular PGA Tour and Senior Tour events without a victory. He won two Senior Tour events in 1991.

THE ONLY FATHER and son to win a major championship were Tom Morris, Sr., and Tom Morris, Jr., who won eight British Opens altogether in the 19th century.

What Goes a Round . . .

It's always nice to have golf balls with your name imprinted on them, but it can be a problem when you lose one. The person finding it doesn't want to use it, and if found by a member of the same golf club, it usually is returned with the original owner having to offer an embarrassed "thank you."

That's not always the case.

Dalton Smith was playing the Longview Golf Course in Greensboro, North Carolina, and lost just such a ball. Eight days later, he was playing at the Pine Tree Golf Course in Kernersville and, while looking for his playing partner's ball, found the one he had lost at Longview, 25 miles away.

The greatest shot in golf is Gene Sarazen's double eagle on the par-5 15th hole to win the 1935 Masters.

HARRY VARDON HAS won the most British Open titles—six.

TOM KITE AND Ben Crenshaw both grew up playing golf at the Country Club of Austin, Texas, where they were taught by Harvey Penick.

THE UNOFFICIAL BIRTH of the Senior PGA Tour was the formation of the Legends of Golf at Onion Creek Country Club in Austin, Texas, in 1978.

THE FIRST SENIOR PGA event was the 1937 PGA Seniors Championship at Augusta National, won by Jock Hutchinson. It wasn't until Arnold Palmer won it in 1980 that victories were considered official Senior PGA Tour titles.

Royal and Ancient Golf Club II

The most famous golf club at St. Andrews is the Royal and Ancient Golf Club. In 1843, another was formed there with the name St. Andrews Mechanics' Golf Club, later renamed the St. Andrews Golf Club, made up of citizens who would probably not have been considered for membership in the R & A. Apparently, they knew how to play the game. A total of 13 of its members won 22 British Opens.

The greatest comeback in the history of golf was Ben Hogan winning the 1950 U.S. Open only 16 months after a severe, near-fatal car wreck in Texas.

The PGA Tour currently ranks Sam Snead as the best golfer in its history with 82 victories. Jack Nicklaus is No. 2 with 73, and Ben Hogan is No. 3 with 64 wins. Fourth-place Arnold Palmer is only two behind with 62. In fifth place and rising is Tiger Woods with 54 wins through the 2006 season.

When rookie golfer Arnold Palmer won the 1955 Canadian Open, he was not allowed to collect any money because he had been on the PGA Tour less than six months, and a player had to be on Tour longer than that to collect cash. That rule was later dumped.

Modern LPGA majors are the U.S. Women's Open, the McDonald's LPGA Championship, the Kraft Nabisco Championship, and the Weetabix Women's British Open. Past majors were the Titleholders Championship, the Western Open, and the du Maurier Ltd. Classic.

To qualify for the LPGA Hall of Fame is the most difficult accomplishment in golf. If a player has won two different majors, she must win at least 30 official events. Players who have won only one major must collect 35 wins. Non-major winners must win 40 tournaments.

Casual Attire

ATTIRE FOR GOLFERS has changed through the years. Even after jackets were no longer being worn, most golfers appeared on the course with long-sleeved white shirts and ties. The first U.S. Open champion to break that tradition was Byron Nelson in 1939, when he wore a short-sleeved, open-necked shirt—the accepted norm for today's golfer.

GEORGE H. W. Bush's grandfather and George W. Bush's great-grandfather, George Herbert Walker, was president of the USGA in the 1920s. The Walker Cup is named after him.

THE SHORTEST HOLE ever played in a major championship is the 107-yard, par-3 7th hole at Pebble Beach.

THE FIRST LADIES golf club in the world was a nine-hole course constructed in 1868 at Westward Ho Golf Club in England.

GOLF'S ORIGINAL "Grand Slam"—U.S. Open, U.S. Amateur, British Open, and British Amateur—was won by Bobby Jones in 1930. He retired after winning it. Nowadays, a Grand Slam would include the U.S. Open, the British Open, the Masters, and the PGA Championship. Tiger Woods is the only golfer to hold each of those championships at the same time, but he accomplished that over two seasons in 2000 and 2001.

MODERN GOLF REALLY became popular in the 1950s because President Eisenhower loved the game, and tournaments on TV showed the world a golfer named Arnold Palmer.

A Big Chunk of Sod

HAVING 185 YARDS left for his second shot at Quaker Ridge Golf Club in Scarsdale, New York, Rick Werner decided to hit a 9-iron. Not too many people can hit a 9-iron that far, but some professionals like Werner have been able to get that kind of distance. What was surprising was the size of the divot. His playing partner, Jim McLean, had it checked out and it measured 22 inches long and 15 inches wide. He swore that the figures were accurate—and that the ball flew over the green.

ACCORDING TO THE USGA Rules of Golf, you are allowed only five minutes to search for a lost ball.

THE FIRST PERMANENT golf club in the United States that is still in existence is St. Andrews Golf Club in New York. It was formed by the Apple Tree Gang in 1888.

THE LONGEST HOLE in the United States is the 841-yard, par-6 12th hole at Meadows Farms Golf Course in Locust Grove, Virginia.

SAM SNEAD IS the oldest winner on the PGA Tour. He was 52 years, 10 months old when he won the 1965 Greater Greensboro Open.

BYRON NELSON HOLDS the PGA Tour record for the most wins in a single season with 18 victories in 1945. Ben Hogan had 13 wins in 1946, and Sam Snead had 11 wins in 1950.

BY WINNING THE Titleholders Championship seven times, the Western Open seven times, and the U.S. Open once, Patty Berg clinched the record for the most LPGA major titles won with 15.

Short Pants

IT IS NO longer unusual for a golfer to have played on both the Walker Cup and Ryder Cup teams during a career. The first to have that distinction, however, was Freddie Haas. Freddie had another first. His victory in the 1945 Memphis Open was as an amateur, and it brought an end to the longest winning streak in PGA history, the 11 straight by Byron Nelson.

Probably because Haas was an amateur, not too many people paid much attention to the fact that he wore shorts during the tournament. It remains the only PGA Tour event on record that was won by a golfer wearing shorts.

ARNOLD PALMER WAS the first player on the PGA Tour to win $1 million in official money.

ARNOLD PALMER AND Jack Nicklaus share the PGA Tour record for the most consecutive years of winning at least one tournament. They each won 17 years in a row.

THE WINNERS OF the most major PGA tournaments make up an elite field. Jack Nicklaus leads with 18, but Tiger Woods, as of the end of the 2006 season, is edging closer to him with 12.

SAM SNEAD IS the only PGA Tour player to shoot better than his age at a Tour event. He shot 66 at age 67 at the 1979 Quad Cities Open.

THE PGA CHAMPIONSHIP was played in match play from 1916 to 1957. The last match-play champion was Lionel Hebert.

THE FIRST WOODEN tee was created in 1920 by Dr. William Lowell, a New Jersey dentist. Before tees were invented, golfers teed up the balls on a tiny wet-sand mound.

ARNOLD PALMER'S FOUR Masters victories came every other year—1958, 1960, 1962, and 1964.

CHARLIE SIFFORD WAS the first black golfer to win a PGA Tour event, the 1967 Hartford Open.

BYRON NELSON WON 11 consecutive PGA Tour tournaments in 1945—possibly the most unbreakable record in all of sports.

ELECTRIC GOLF CARTS were first introduced into the world of golf in the late 1950s. Now more than 90 percent of all golfers in the United States ride in carts.

THE OLDEST PLAYER to win a major championship was 48-year-old Julius Boros at the 1968 PGA Championship.